ORGANIC GARDENING IN THE AMERICAN WEST

Raising Vegetables in a Short, Dry, Growing Season

by
Robert F. Smith, Jr.

SUNSTONE PRESS

SANTA FE

Cover art by Kris Hotvedt

© 1999 by Robert F. Smith, Jr.
All rights reserved.

Printed and bound in the United States of America. No part of this book may be reproduced in any form or by any electronic or mechanical means including information storage and retrieval systems, without permission in writing from the publisher, except by a reviewer who may quote brief passages in a review.

Sunstone books may be purchased for educational, business, or sales promotional use. For information please write: Special Markets Department, Sunstone Press, P.O. Box 2321, Santa Fe, New Mexico 87504-2321.

REVISED EDITION

Library of Congress Cataloging in Publication Data:

Smith, Robert F. (Robert Farquharson), 1931–
    Organic gardening in the American West: raising vegetables in a short, dry, growing season / by Robert F. Smith, Jr. —Rev. ed
       p. cm.
    Rev. ed. of: Organic gardening in the West. c1976
    ISBN: 0-86534-282-2
    1. Vegetable gradening—West (U.S.) 2. Organic gardening—West (U.S.) I. Smith, Robert F. (Robert Farquharson), 1931– Organic gardening in the West. II. Title.
SB324. 3. S64   1998
635′ .0484′ 0978—dc   98-29430
                                                        CIP

Published by   SUNSTONE PRESS
                       Post Office Box 2321
                       Santa Fe, NM 87504-2321 / USA
                       (505) 988-4418 / *orders only* (800) 243-5644
                       FAX (505) 988-1025

TABLE OF CONTENTS

Foreword 5
Introduction 7
    Tools 9
    Planning the Garden 11
    Making Beds 13
    Fertilizers and Composts 16
    Soil Preparation 19
    Cold Frame 22
    Seeds 24
    Starting Plants in Flats 25
    Transplanting 27
    Planting Directly in the Garden 28
    Mulching 29
    Irrigation 30
    Weeding 36
    Pests 36
    Adverse Weather Conditions 39
    Selling Produce 41
    Culture of Specific Crops:
        asparagus 46
        green beans 48
        beets 50
        broccoli 51

brussels sprouts	52
cabbage	53
carrots	55
cauliflower	58
celeriac	59
chives	60
sweet corn	61
cucumbers	63
garlic	65
horse beans	66
horse radish	67
kale	68
kohlrabi	68
lettuce	69
multiplier onions	71
onions	72
parsley	74
peas	75
potatoes	77
pumpkins	79
radishes	81
rhubarb	83
shallots	85
sorrel	86
spinach	87
squash	88
strawberries	90
sunflowers	92
swiss chard	93
tomatoes	94
turnips	96

FOREWORD
from the first edition

Though I had cultivated a small backyard vegetable patch for several years, it wasn't until the late 1960's, while living in Berkeley, California, that I became a full-time gardener. The place was People's Park Annex, spontaneously created on a half block of transit district property during the height of student demonstrations around the University of California. The Annex was not a promising place for gardening. A subway had recently been built there and the construction trench had been filled with clay. The original top soil had been scraped off and used for landscaping elsewhere.

Before good vegetables and flowers could be grown, the soil had to be loosened to allow air and water to penetrate it. This was achieved by incorporating generous amounts of compost in the soil. I learned from Lucy Hupp, a long-time organic gardener, to dispense with spading the ground and to cultivate the soil with a simple, rocking motion of the fork instead. She also taught me to plant in depressed beds rather than on conventional ridges. Though irrigation water ran right over the plants, they were not washed out. Instead they thrived, protected from the drying wind that swept in from the west. Using these techniques, we quickly succeeded with cool season crops, like beets and lettuce, which were suitable to a maritime climate. Fortunately pests were rare; snails had been destroyed by the original clearing of the land, and it was a year before they reappeared in the park.

Though I was pleased with my results, the desire to farm and garden on a larger scale than possible in Berkeley became stronger and stronger, and in 1970 my family and I were delighted to move to land in northern New Mexico on the eastern slope of the Sangre de Cristo mountains. Through the farm ran a small valley with two acres of gently sloping, alluvial soil. A well nearby would supply the water.

But the new location brought with it new problems. The cool summers were like those in the Bay Area, but the growing season was far shorter. Instead of 300 days, it was only 120. Frosts could occur until the end of May, and the first fall frost was sometimes as early as September 10. I had to learn to grow our vegetables within these limits, though the season could be extended by using a cold frame and by protecting the plants when frosts threatened.

Insects were much more of a challenge than they had been in California. Gone were the hungry snails, but in their place were white grubs, flea beetles and the harlequin bug. Since I was committed to organic gardening, I had to learn to cope with these insects without using chemical pesticides.

At first I tried to grow all the vegetables that our family liked, but in a year or two I came to realize that it was wasted effort to grow crops that needed a climate different from ours. For example, watermelons and cantaloupes would not ripen, regardless of what varieties we used. They needed hot days and warm nights, the opposite of what we have. So I reluctantly gave them up and concentrated on plants more suitable to our climate.

This fall I have harvested my fifth garden in New Mexico. My experiences both in California and in New Mexico will, I hope, make this book a helpful one for you, gardening in the mountains and dry plains of the west.

I wish to thank Joan Strachanowski for information for the article on cauliflower, and John Ellefson for material on Jerusalem artichokes and multiplier onions, and for comments on the rest of the book. Julia Smith gave much time to studying the manuscript and offered numerous suggestions for improving both content and style. David Smith made many helpful criticisms. To them I also offer my appreciation.

Robert F. Smith Jr.
... near San Geronimo, New Mexico, September 1975.

INTRODUCTION

Many gardening books are already in print and more are published every month, but they are not written with the mountain garden and climate in mind. Most books are based upon knowledge of the eastern half of the nation, with its wet springs and hot summers. But gardening in a short, dry growing season is unique and deserves special consideration. Here on the eastern slope of the southern Rockies, for instance, our dry, windy springs, cool summers, and untimely frosts demand special gardening practices that are not covered by gardening books now in print. This book attempts to fill the gap.

Another unique feature of this book is that it describes methods for laying out garden beds and preparing the soil which are not only adapted to our climate, but also energy-saving, no small consideration when you are doing a large garden with hand tools.

I have been as specific as possible so that the beginner following my instructions should be successful right from the start. Included, for instance, is information about the fertilizer and water needs for each vegetable to insure their rapid growth. Armed with these instructions, the reader should find no insurmountable obstacle to successful organic gardening. He should be able easily to locate abundant and inexpensive sources of natural fertilizers. Noxious insects can be controlled by handpicking or by careful choice of planting date. At the very worst, you might have to omit a vegetable because it cannot resist an insect or disease, but you can usually find a successful substitute.

I have omitted describing how to grow vegetables that do poorly in our climate. Our days and nights are too cool to produce a good crop of eggplant, peppers, or melons. They could be grown using a greenhouse, but, for us anyway, they are not worth the effort or expense.

The tools are hand tools. They are adequate, if well-maintained and employed efficiently, for gardens up to one-half acre in size. Unlike complex machines, good hand tools will last many years with only the occasional replacement of a wooden handle.

I welcome comments about the book, and I hope to receive specific information about seeds and gardening techniques adapted to our climate. Eventually these new ideas will be incorporated into a revised edition.

TOOLS

If your garden is smaller than 1,000 square feet, then hand tools are all you will ever need for soil preparation, planting, and weeding. Even one-half acre is not too great an area for hand tools, provided they are used intelligently and kept in good condition. For a larger plot, however, a horse, tractor, or rototiller is necessary. Our half-acre garden takes up at least half our time during May and June when planting is being done and irrigation needs are greatest. When the rainy season arrives, work slacks off to pick up again during the harvest.

Buy the best tools you can afford, and maintain them well. Cheap equipment is poorly made and falls apart quickly. To keep tools from splitting, oil the handles at the beginning and the end of the gardening season. Old crankcase oil is perfect. Put on a thick coat, and allow it to soak in before wiping off the excess. Do not leave the tools stuck in the ground, but shelter them from dirt, rain, and sun. To prevent rust, brush off dirt after each use. Above all, keep tools sharp. A sharp hoe will slice through the weeds with one easy stroke, while a dull hoe makes the same task slow and tedious.

The following equipment is essential for hand gardening:

A spading fork, preferably long-handled for more leverage and less stooping. Since this kind is hard to find, however, you will probably have to settle for a D-handled one. Check to see that the head is securely fastened to the shaft and that the handle grip is large enough to be comfortable in the hand. Do not overtax the fork. Even the strongest tines will bend if you attempt to cultivate hard, dry soil. Wait until it rains or irrigate the ground the day before.

A manure fork, for handling manure and compost. Do not use it for cultivating, or the tines will bend.

A flat-nosed shovel. Use this versatile tool to make beds. When well-sharpened, it will scrape off young weeds with a minimum of effort. It is also essential for moving manure, dirt, and sand.

A long-handled spade, for digging holes. Keep it sharpened with a file.

A rake, to smooth beds for planting. Buy one with the head attached to the handle with pieces of curved steel rod.

A garden hoe. Get the best one you can afford. Invaluable for close-in weeding and for making seed drills. Sharpen it before every use.

A wheel hoe for digging trenches for planting potatoes and large seeds like corn and peas. The cultivator attachment can be used for the final preparation of the beds after they have been forked.

A wheelbarrow, though expensive, is a necessity for all large gardens. It provides the only feasible way to move large amounts of manure and compost. Buy one with at least a four cubic foot capacity, with large oak handles, and an inflatable tire.

A sheet or bed spread. You can carry an amazing amount of grass clippings or leaves in a large cloth slung over the shoulder.

A garden trowel. Essential for digging small holes for transplanting. Most cheap trowels bend at the neck so search for one that has a strong joint between blade and handle.

A small spatula. Invaluable for blocking and lifting transplants from boxes. A two-inch size is sufficient.

A scale that will weigh up to sixty pounds, to determine yields objectively. It is easy to exaggerate your gardening successes.

A bastard file, for sharpening tools.

A wire brush, for scraping dirt off the implements.

PLANNING THE GARDEN

The ideal location for a garden is near your house, close to water, in full sun but sheltered from the wind, and on deep, well-drained soil sloping slightly to the south. A garden near the house is better cared for than one far away. It can be watched, and insects or rodents controlled before they do serious damage. The gardener will spend more time there since it is convenient to work in during his spare minutes.

All vegetables need at least six hours of full sun a day. Even cool season crops like peas and cabbage must have direct sun though they cannot take intense heat. Keep the edge of the garden at least four or five feet away from the outermost branches of trees and shrubs, which not only shade the vegetables but also compete for water and nutrients.

In deep, friable soil, plants are vigorous and drought-resistant since their roots go deep and draw moisture and fertilizer from a greater volume of soil than if confined to a shallow surface layer. If drainage is poor and water stands on the ground for days at a time, most plants will sicken and die.

Shelter the garden from the spring wind which erodes the soil, dries out the ground, and injures the plants. If no barrier to the wind exists, plant a row of fast-growing trees like the native plum; or, if space is limited, try a hedge of roses and harvest a crop of hips in the fall.

But who is fortunate enough to have a garden that satisfies all these conditions? Ours is located in a small valley with good soil and available water, but our house is far away and the wind howls through the garden in the spring. Because cold air settles in the valley, frost damage commonly occurs in late spring and early fall. But at our house, only 200 feet above the garden, the growing season is two weeks longer; unfortunately the soil is shallow and there is no water.

So choose your garden site carefully. Availability of water and good soil are most important. To check your soil, dig down with a spade or post hole digger to where topsoil turns into subsoil. Top soil is usually dark and loose in texture. Subsoil is heavy and lighter-colored. If the top layer is less than a foot deep, gardening will be difficult. Roots will tend to remain near the surface and the plants will need frequent waterings. To improve such soil, remove the top soil with a spade, and fork in at least three inches of compost in the exposed subsoil beneath. Then replace the top soil. But this is heavy work. It is better to choose another site with better soil, if, that is, one is available.

Once the site has been chosen, the next step is to plan the garden. Which vegetables you grow is basically a matter of taste (within the limitations imposed by the climate). Space allotted to each vegetable depends on individual need and potential crop yield. Yields for some crops are easy to calculate. For instance, 50 feet of lettuce, with plants spaced six inches apart, will produce 100 heads, a lot of lettuce. Other vegetables, like peas, are less predictable, and you have to learn from experience what to expect. Summer squash almost always makes more fruit than you can use, regardless of how little is planted.

Be sure to leave plenty of room between beds so that you can work without stepping on the plants. On flat ground, beds can be made as wide as desired, so long as you can reach to their centers from either side. But on a slope they should be narrow. Otherwise too high a bank must be built up on the lower side to hold water and too much soil must be scraped away from the higher side to make the bed level.

Grow tall plants, like corn and sunflowers, at the north end of the garden where they will not shade shorter crops. If your beds run north and south, put tall vegetables at the west end, where they will act as a wind shield. Also, short plants at the east end receive more sun, since during the rainy season mornings tend to be clear and afternoons cloudy.

In reality, the actual garden plan must be a compromise among various needs. Most crops should be rotated each year, and, in spite of the best intentions, tall plants must sometimes be put at the south end of the garden and heat-sensitive vegetables end up with a south exposure.

Crop rotation should lead to a more economical use of fertilizer. Beds that have been heavily manured for a heavy feeder like cabbage will grow a good crop of peas with the addition of only a little wood ashes. The need for nitrogen of peas will be satisfied by the carry-over of manure the second year.

Rotation also helps control soil insects and diseases by removing them from where plants pests have built up. If related crops are not grown in the same place for several years, most of the insects and disease organisms that afflict them will die off.

MAKING BEDS

Growing vegetables in depressed beds, which I am about to describe, is just the opposite of the usual practice. Plants are usually raised on ridges with irrigation water running in trenches between them. In this way, the soil is well-aerated, and it warms up fast in the spring.

When springs are wet and the drainage poor, the usual method is justified, but in our semi-arid climate, with spring winds and persistent drought, depressed planting without separate irrigation trenches is to be preferred. The soil stays moist longer, and beds are protected from the winds by the ridges between them. Because of good drainage, high evaporation, and dry air, we never have a problem with plants being too wet. The ridges also serve as paths so you never need to walk on the growing area itself.

Before beds can be made, weeds should be raked away and thrown on the compost heap. Then dig out the roots of perennial weeds like sweet clover and mallow. Do a thorough job; for after the garden is up, pulling well-established weeds often takes your vegetables with them. Small annual weeds can be scraped off with a flat-nosed shovel.

In cross section a typical depressed bed looks like this:

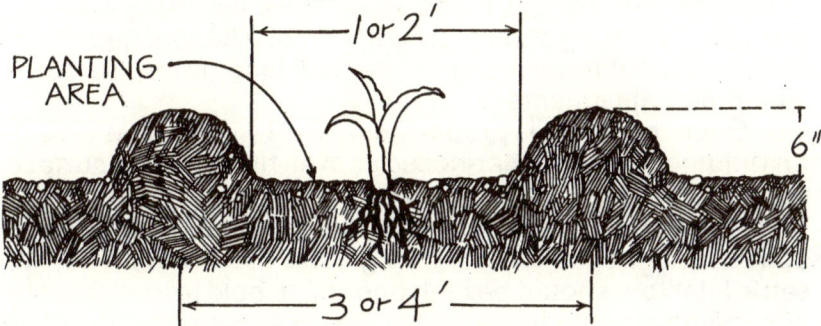

The ridges should be high enough so that they will hold several inches of water. The width of the flat area depends on whether you are growing one or more than one row in a bed. If one row is planted, then the planted area should be one foot wide. If two or three rows are sown, two feet is the proper width. (In the rest of the book, a narrow bed means a one-foot bed, a wide bed a two-foot bed.) The distance from center to center of the ridges will be either three or four feet.

We must lay out beds so that water will flow evenly over the whole surface without causing erosion or plant washout. Beds no longer than 25 feet can be level, but longer ones must be gently sloped. Our garden has a drop of no more than three inches per 50-foot bed. Such a slope is a good compromise between speed and thoroughness of watering. With a one-inch plastic hose, water moves fast enough to quickly cover 25 feet of bed; thus the hose must be moved only once per bed. Beds with a greater slope are difficult to water because water runs off faster than it soaks in. It could collect and overflow the lower end of the bed.

Take plenty of time to dig out beds with the right slope. Later, when the seedlings are up and you discover that the beds do not water right, it will be too late to correct the slope.

For leveling, you need a line level, available at hardware stores for a little more than a dollar, and about 75 feet of strong string. Pound in a two-foot stake at each end of the bed and fasten the string between the stakes. Pull it tight to eliminate sagging. To get a true reading, hang the level at the exact center of the string. Move the string up or down one stake until it is level. Compare the string with the ground beneath. If the lay of the land differs much from the line, then move one stake up or down the slope and adjust the string to maintain a level position. With the string parallel to the ground, less dirt will have to be moved to build the bed.

If the beds are less than 25 feet, leave the string level, but if longer, the string should be sloped. For a 50-foot bed, either raise or lower it three inches. Other bed lengths require corresponding adjustments.

Once the string is properly sloped, it will serve as a guide for digging. Using the flat-nosed shovel, first even the surface, scraping off the high places and filling the low ones. Then remove three inches of dirt and place along the edges of the bed to make ridges six inches high and a foot wide. They will settle later, but should be high enough to hold irrigation water after being repeatedly walked on. Refer to your planting chart to decide if beds should be one or two feet wide.

Once a bed is graded, simply shift each stake ahead three or four feet to the next bed. Put up the string, level it, and adjust one end up or down for slope. Then dig the bed, using the string as a guide. If the garden site is flat or has an even slope, you can dig the beds with only an occasional use of the level, but if the surface is irregular, then the level should be checked for each bed.

Do not cultivate the ground before making the beds. Wait until they have been leveled and manured. But if the ground is very hard or covered with a tough turf, and you have a tractor or rototiller, one pass with the machine will make the work a lot easier.

Remember to make ridges high enough. They will settle to half their original height. If too low, water will run from one bed to the next and can erode the planted area, especially on a steeply sloping site.

Beds are easiest to make when the soil is moist, so get them done before the soil dries out in the spring. But if the soil is hard, give it a good soaking and it will be ready to dig in a couple of days.

FERTILIZERS AND COMPOSTS

An excellent garden can be grown with cheap natural fertilizers obtained from local stables, dairies, or sewer plants. A pickup load will be free or will cost no more than a few dollars, and some places will even load your truck for you. Some organic gardeners have recommended using fertilizers like cottonseed meal, but lately they have become very expensive. Stick to the cheaper ones.

Before loading the manure into your truck, look the pile over carefully and take the well-rotted stuff. Aged manure is free of cakes and uniform in consistency. A shovel easily penetrates it. In a barn, however, even aged manure will be hard because animals have compressed it. Though the quality is excellent, you may have to break it loose with a pick.

If you don't have a truck, borrow or rent a trailer for a day and make several trips. Remember to get plenty since the average garden needs about a full pickup load for every two hundred running feet of bed.

Aged animal manure is the best natural fertilizer. It is a complete plant food and adds humus to the soil. But if you can't get manure, or if it is too expensive, sewer sludge is a good substitute. If well-aged, it is completely safe to use since disease-producing germs are destroyed as it composts.

Every community has its pile of sludge, and it should be easy to find. Go directly to the sewer plant to get permission to take the sludge. It is a lot quicker than working through the city bureaucracy. Many communities give it away free, some charge a small fee, and others, unfortunately, use it for land fill or even dump it into the ocean.

The best sludge is soft and slightly moist. Dry sludge often comes in rock-like chunks which are hard to incorporate in the soil. For ease of use and safety, all sludge should go through a composting process in the garden which will both improve its texture and kill any disease germs that might be present. So obtain it in the fall and age it over the winter in a flat-topped pile several feet high. Make a ridge around the edge to hold rainwater or melting snow, and by spring it should be well-broken down. If the rains are unreliable, soak the pile once in the fall with a hose.

As a final safety measure, do not use sludge for any root crop which is eaten raw, like garlic, carrots, or radishes. But it is safe to grow root crops in soil sludged the previous year because any pathogenic organisms present will have been destroyed by the soil's natural composting processes. Since sewer sludge lacks potassium and is low in phosphorus it should be supplemented. Fortunately, wood ashes from your fire place contain both these elements. Use the white ash which is completely burned. Black pieces of wood or paper contain unburned carbon which ties up soil nitrogen until it is decomposed. Screen the ashes through one-half inch hardware cloth, or its equivalent, to remove metal or glass. Protect them from rain which will leach out potassium. Wood ashes are alkaline, so they should not be used on potatoes which are attacked by scab in alkaline soils.

If you get manure from your own farm animals, the best practice is to haul it from the barn directly to the garden and immediately incorporate it into the garden soil. Do not leave manure (or sludge for that matter) lying on top of the beds, for it will lose half its nitrogen in a few days from leaching and direct loss to the air. If manure must be stored outside, make a large compact pile, or, better yet, store it in an underground pit, covered with plastic, weighted down against the wind.

Besides its great value as a fertilizer, compost adds filler to the soil which helps keep it from crusting. Some crops, like radishes, really respond to its use. Gathering materials and building the pile take a lot of time, but the results are worth it. Start your pile in the spring, at least six weeks before the garden is to be planted. A pile made in early fall will be ready the following spring.

To build a compost heap, spread a layer of vegetable matter, six feet square and six inches thick, on a bare, flat piece of ground. Use grass clippings and green succulent weeds. Avoid woody stems or dried, brown plants, which lack nitrogen and take longer to decay. Weeds gone to seed are also less nutritious, and the seeds will germinate when the compost is used unless they are destroyed by the heat of decomposition. Put kitchen garbage, except for egg shells and bones, in the center of the pile and it will break down fast and not be disturbed by dogs. Do not pack down the materials or add dirt. Air must penetrate the pile for hot decomposition to take place.

On the first layer of vegetable matter, spread two inches of manure or sludge and a sprinkling of wood ashes (or some other source of phosphorus, like bonemeal, to prevent nitrogen loss). Keep the pile as level as possible. Continue alternating six-inch layers of vegetation and two-inch layers of manure and wood ashes until the pile is at least five feet tall. Keep the edges as close to vertical as possible. Build a ridge around the edge to hold any rain or melting snow, and wet the whole pile so that it is damp but not soaked.

If the pile is built right and the weather warm, it should heat up promptly. After three or four days the center of the heap should be almost too hot to touch. If the center is cold or barely warm, decomposition will be slow, and it may take six months for the compost to be usable in the garden. But if it really heats up, it will be ready after six weeks, though still coarse and fibrous. Turning the pile after several weeks bring about uniform decomposition.

Covering the pile is not necessary; in fact, it will actually slow decomposition. Nor is a container essential. If built with a wide enough base, the pile will be self-supporting. Also, a free-standing pile is easier to turn, and a box or container costs considerable money.

SOIL PREPARATION

The best time to prepare the soil is in the spring several weeks before planting. Manure will quickly break down in the soil and plant roots will not be damaged by contact with fresh manure. Fall preparation is risky because strong winds could erode the soil.

The soil in the beds should be prepared in a definite sequence. First sprinkle wood ashes on the planting surface (if they are needed). Do this on a calm day. A strong wind will blow them all over the garden before they can be dug in.

Once the ashes are spread, immediately cover them with manure or sludge. Using a wheelbarrow, dump small piles in the bed and then rake them out until the layer is even. It takes two to three wheel barrow loads to cover a 50 × 2-foot bed to a depth of one inch.

To dig in the fertilizer, start at one end of the bed, force the spading fork straight into the ground and pull back vigorously on the handle to burst open the ground and allow manure to sift into the broken earth. Move backwards in the bed, take another bite about six inches from the first and again open the soil. Proceed in this fashion until the end of the bed is reached. Then, walking along the ridge, fork the bed again but this time at right angles to the initial cultivation.

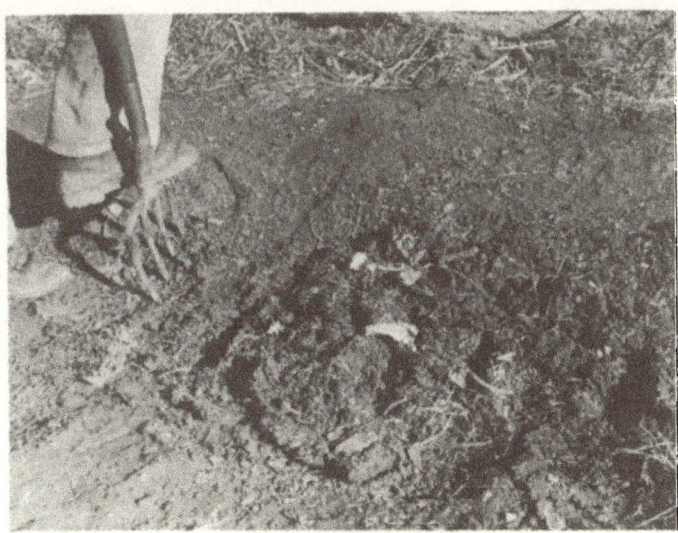

The fork is about to be pushed into the earth. Notice that it is perpendicular to the ground.

With the fork sunk in the ground the handle is pushed sharply down, bursting open the soil and allowing fertilizer to sift into the earth.

Clumps are broken up with the back of the fork. A hoe can also be used here.

The last step in soil preparation is raking the soil free of lumps.

This method of digging beds is both consistent with the growth habits of plants and easy on the back. It keeps most of the manure near the surface which creates an especially fertile medium for the shallow roots of young plants. When the roots are older and tougher, they will easily penetrate the harder soil underneath. This method imitates nature's way, which leaves a rich layer of rotting vegetable matter on the surface. Most important it is much less work than lifting and turning the earth, for mechanical advantage is gained through the rocking motion.

If the ground is too dry to fork, water the bed or wait for a soaking rain. Then let the soil dry a little before forking. If it is too wet when cultivated, it will form rock-like chunks which when dry are hard to break up. In our silty soil, a two days' wait is sufficient, but clay soil would take longer.

The final step is to break up any remaining clods into pieces a half inch or smaller. The degree of cultivation depends upon the size of seeds being planted. Carrots require the finest of soils whereas corn only needs a coarse cultivation. For a small garden, use the back of the fork, a rake, or a hand cultivator. A wheel hoe cultivator is required for the large garden.

Using this method you can prepare several hundred feet of bed in a day. It is good exercise too.

COLD FRAME

With a longer growing season, we could seed all our crops directly in the ground, but with only about 115 days between killing frosts, plants must have a head start. With a cold frame, tender varieties can be started about two months earlier than is usually safe. Early varieties of tomatoes begun indoors about March 1, and transplanted to the garden around June 1, will ripen starting the middle of July. The cold frame will also extend the season of hardy plants, like lettuce, into the late fall. A cold frame needs a warm, sunny but sheltered location which is near the house and close to water. It must be checked several times a day, and during warm weather the plants need water twice a day.

The south side of a house is an ideal location, if it receives full sun. The house wall, which becomes the back of the cold frame, traps and reflects the heat of the sun. It also shelters the plants from cold north air. Another good place is the south side of a hill. If neither type of site is available, however, a cold frame can be dug on flat ground although it is not as warm, and part of the growing space will be shaded by the front edge of the excavation.

For the past three years we have used a cold frame dug into a south-facing hill. It is covered with two layers of four mil polyethylene film supported on 6 × 6 wire mesh. The opening is ten feet by ten feet with the back wall about two feet high. The rear half of the floor is elevated about six inches above the front half. We piled rocks against the walls to reinforce them, and ridged dirt above the back wall to divert any run-off water.

The covers were made like this:

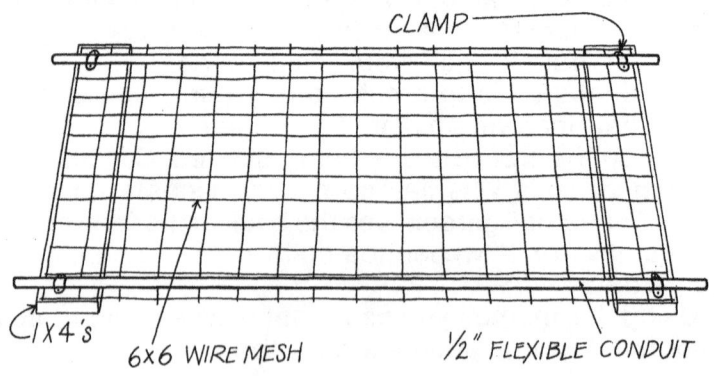

Plastic was wrapped around the frame, stapled to the end boards and kept in place with string wound around the cover at two foot intervals. Though a crude type of cover, it was inexpensive and protected the tender plants even when the night-time temperature fell as low as 19 degrees. Rocks at the corners kept the covers from blowing off in the spring winds.

Although this type of cover worked satisfactorily for three years, it had certain disadvantages. It took two people to open and close it. The plastic cover had to be replaced every year, for wind ripped the plastic loose, and hail storms shredded the film.

A really durable cover should be built from glass or fiberglass, but these are expensive materials. We managed to locate four used windows with their panes intact for two dollars each at a junk yard. Hinged to the south side of the house, they make a cold frame 15 feet long by three feet wide. Normally the top should be protected from hail with one-half inch hardware cloth, but we can leave it uncovered since the house shields it from damaging hail which usually blows in from the north.

A cold frame needs constant attention. Even on a cool day, intense sunlight can produce temperatures over 100 degrees in a closed cold frame and damage heat-sensitive plants like lettuce or cabbage. So put a thermometer inside and check it several times a day when the top is closed. When the temperature rises above 80 degrees, the top should be opened.

Group together plants that need heat like tomatoes and peppers and keep them covered on cooler days.

On mild days the cold frame can be opened around ten in the morning and left open until four in the afternoon. When closed, the cover traps heat absorbed during the day and keeps the cold frame warmer at night. If you are going to be away for a day or two, cover the top with tarps or blankets to keep the sun out.

In late spring, you might be tempted to leave the cover open on frost-free nights, but birds foraging at dawn and dusk will eat the plants, especially if there are no other green plants nearby. Watch for signs of rodent damage. In the spring of 1974, during a rodent population explosion, we lost whole flats of plants until we killed the mice in traps baited with cheese and grain.

SEEDS

Ninety percent of fresh seed bought from reputable companies should germinate, but older seed will vary in viability, depending on type, age, and storage conditions. Seeds good for only one or two years are corn, leeks, onion, and parsley. Those you can expect to live for three to five years are asparagus, beans, Brussels sprouts, cabbage, carrots, cauliflower, kale, lettuce, peas, radish, spinach, and turnip. Cucumber and tomato seeds might last five years.

Old seeds, or those of unknown age, should be given a germination test. On a damp piece of paper towel or white cloth, sprinkle a representative sample of at least 20 seeds. Roll up the cloth or paper tightly, place in a plastic bag, and fasten the end. Leave in a warm place for a week or longer, depending on the variety of seed. Then open the package and count the seeds that have sprouted. If 15 out of 20 have germinated, the rate is 75 percent. Once the rate is determined, then you will know how thickly to sow seed to bring up the required stand of plants.

Store seeds in the coolest and driest part of the house, preferably a north room, and away from stoves and heating vents. Keep them in covered glass or metal containers to prevent insect or rodent damage.

STARTING PLANTS IN FLATS

Flats can be built cheaply out of scrap lumber. Two-by-fours make especially durable sides which resist warping and splitting, but one by fours are adequate, and they reduce the weight of the box. Plywood is best for the bottom, but inch boards will work also. A good size is 12 by 18 inches, inside dimensions. It will hold about 50 plants when they are spaced two inches apart. Larger sizes are too heavy. If the bottom is solid, drill about six one-half inch holes for drainage. Cover them with aluminum screening, or stuff with rocks, to keep the soil from sifting out.

First nail the sides together, using sixteen penny box nails for two by fours and eight penny box nails for one inch boards. Then nail on the bottom with eight penny nails.

Make a rich soil mixture to insure rapid plant growth. A good formula is one-third compost or rotted manure, one-third top soil, and one-third sand. Choose the ingredients from a place where flea beetles have not been active. If their eggs are present, they will hatch out in the boxes and attack members of the cabbage family.

Sift the mixture through a quarter-inch screen and wet it thoroughly before putting it in the boxes. Massage the soil with your hands to make sure it is completely damp, since it repels water when dry and could stay that way if not forcibly dampened.

Fill the flats within a half-inch of the top, press the soil level with a board, and you are ready to plant. Furrows are quickly and uniformly made with the edge of a one-fourth inch board cut a little shorter than the box. Press the edge into the soil to the required depth, sprinkle the seeds in the drill and fill with extra moistened soil. Rows can be made every one or two inches and the plants later thinned to one or two inches depending on the variety. Water with a sprinkling can and cover with plastic. The soil should stay moist until the seeds germinate, but check every few days to make sure. Keep boxes in a warm place until the seedlings appear. Then uncover the flats and move them immediately to the cold frame. Do not delay. In the dark, seedlings quickly become lanky, and will topple over when transplanted.

Thin seedlings, after they have their true leaves, to give them plenty of room to grow and to allow air to circulate around them. Water in the morning so that the surface of the soil will have a chance to dry out during the day. If the plants are not growing rapidly, or if the color is not dark-green, sprinkle a half-inch of well-rotted manure on the surface to speed up growth.

If you only raise a few plants, and a flat is too large, use small tin cans or plastic yogurt containers. Open two holes with a can opener at the bottom edge of the sides or cut holes with scissors in plastic containers. Cover the bottom with small rocks and fill to a half-inch of the top with the planting mixture. Otherwise, care is the same as for flats.

Damping off is sometimes a problem, especially with tomato plants. It is a fungus disease which attacks plants near their base and causes them to fall over and die. Damping off in tomatoes can be prevented by pouring boiling water through the soil in the flat. For other plants, good gardening practice will control this disease. Thin seedlings promptly to give them plenty of light and air. Give flats direct sun whenever possible, and water early in the day so the soil surface has a chance to dry out.

TRANSPLANTING

The goal of transplanting is to transfer plants from flat to garden with a minimum of damage and setback. The only tools needed for transplanting are a small kitchen spatula and a garden trowel.

To reduce transplant shock, block out young plants two weeks before placing them in the garden. With the spatula slice through the soil around each plant clear to the bottom of the flat. It is just like cutting a cake. Because the roots are confined to each section, later the whole unit will be easy to lift out intact. For a few days you should water more since many roots have been cut.

For transplanting, the flat should be damp. When too wet, the blocked-out plants will be hard to handle; if dry, they may fall apart. A flat watered in the morning should be just right by afternoon. For transplanting in the morning, water the previous night.

Cool, cloudy weather is ideal for transplanting. The plant's need for water is reduced and it is less likely to wilt. If you must transplant during hot, dry weather, the evening hours are best.

Lift a blocked-out plant with the spatula and carefully place it in a previously dug hole. Set the plant slightly below ground level and it will be easier to water. Pack dirt around it so that all air spaces are filled. This is the most important step. Air pockets will dry out and kill exposed roots. Water in further to settle the soil and get the plants established.

In hot, dry weather, the plants need water every day for at least a week. If they wilt badly, cover with cans or pots during the heat of the day. Remove the covers at night or crickets will crawl in to eat the plants.

If you do not wish to use flats, you can grow plants at one end of a bed and transplant them to fill the row. The soil is hard to hold together around the roots so there will be more shock than when transplanting from flats.

Grow more transplants than you need since some will inevitably be lost. Any left over can be given away.

PLANTING DIRECTLY IN THE GARDEN

We plant twice as many seeds as we want plants. This degree of overplanting allows for germination failure and insect and disease loss. To plant large seeds, like corn or beans, dig a trench to the required depth with a hoe or wheel hoe. If the soil is damp, enough moisture should be present to bring up the seed without further watering. If the ground is dry at planting time, irrigate the bed a day or two beforehand. After a shower the soil surface can crust, and even large seed will not be able to break through. To keep a crust from forming, mulch the rows immediately after planting, or keep the surface moist by watering until the rows come up. You can break the crust with a rake, but be careful not to damage the seedlings just under the surface.

To plant small seeds, dig a shallow drill with a stick or hoe. The depth varies from a quarter-inch for the smallest seeds to a half-inch for larger ones. Take a pinch of seeds with the thumb and index finger and sprinkle evenly in the drill, leaving several to the inch. Pull dirt over the row and firm with the back of a rake or hoe. If dry, the bed should be watered deeply prior to planting. Keep the soil moist until the seedlings emerge. In hot, dry, or windy weather this means sprinkling every two or three days, even when the row is covered with mulch. Unmulched beds need daily waterings during such times. Be sure to pull away any mulch as soon as the seeds germinate. Otherwise, they will grow lanky and rarely make sturdy plants.

MULCHING

We use mulches selectively in our garden. Though our summers are mild with air temperatures rarely reaching 90 degrees, the intense radiation from the sun at 7,000 feet heats the soil up, so we keep a permanent deep mulch around plants which grow well only in cool soil, like potatoes, cabbage, and peas. But heat-loving plants such as corn and cucumbers are left unmulched. The sun also dries out seed beds rapidly unless covered with a light mulch until the seeds germinate.

Mulch serves as a hiding place for insects, so check your young plants often for damage. Pull the mulch away if many are being eaten.

Popular mulching materials, like spoiled hay, are not available here, so we use pine needles, gathered from flat areas around the house. Needles are not taken from hillsides because the bare earth could easily erode in heavy rains. Pine needles make a long-lasting mulch which stays in place because the needles interlock. Still, we have to cover them with boards in the spring because of the winds. If weeds are not composted, they can be tucked in around plants as they are pulled.

Whatever material you use, make sure it will not interfere with irrigating in depressed beds. Bark, for instance, impedes the flow of water. But it is excellent to use around plants grown individually or in hills which are watered one at a time.

IRRIGATION

Irrigating a large garden is a time-consuming activity. Hoses must be shifted from one bed to the next, but not before each has received an adequate soaking. At the same time we must be careful that no seedlings are washed out or tender plants crushed by the weight of the hoses. So who does not yearn for the rainy season to start, after weeks of watering under the clear spring sky? Hopes begin to rise when the first thunderheads build up over the mountains to the west, but they often yield only a few sprinkles. We must wait until July for heavy rains to come, and some years, even that doesn't happen.

Frequency of irrigation varies with the weather, type of soil, variety and size of the plant, but whatever the conditions, it should be done evenly and deeply. Shallow watering, even though frequently done, wets only the top few inches of soil. To survive, plants must concentrate their roots near the surface where they can dry out and die during a drought. Plants that are forced, by infrequent but thorough waterings, to root deeply are healthy and drought-resistant.

But irrigation should not be so heavy that water sinks beyond the deepest roots. Water is not only wasted, but valuable nitrogen and potassium are leached away and lost.

So match the depth of water to the needs of the plants. Roots of young plants are shallow, only extending a few inches into the soil, so they need frequent and shallow watering. Mature roots penetrate down to five feet, though the active roots of most well-established plants are concentrated in the top two feet of soil. Hence they require deeper but less frequent irrigations than do young plants.

Signs that plants need water vary from the obvious to the quite subtle. Lettuce wilts when its roots cannot draw enough water from the soil. Corn leaf margins roll when stressed for water, whereas plants like beans just grow more slowly and have smaller pods.

But a garden should be watered before it shows signs of drought. Plants literally work to take in water. By the time they show signs of deprivation, they are putting all their energy into finding moisture and very little is left for growth. To be sure that plants get sufficient water, establish an irrigation schedule and stick to it.

Most of the water roots take from the soil is evaporated from the leaves. This process seems wasteful, but evaporation keeps leaves from overheating and surrounds them with a layer of moist air. So on days that are clear, dry, and windy, plants need many times as much water as in cloudy, still, or damp weather.

Rainfall amounts are easy to overestimate without an objective measurement, so a rain gauge is a useful garden tool. Light showers add little to a plant's water supply. They only wet the plant or dampen the surface of the ground. If the showers amount to several tenths of an inch or more, and occur on consecutive days, they can be considered cumulative. But if separated by several days of hot weather, they have little effect.

If the weather has been hot, clear, windy and rainless since the last irrigation, large, rapidly growing plants need a heavy watering which will saturate the top two feet of soil. To determine how deep the water penetrates, push a piece of reinforcing rod in the ground until it meets noticeable resistance. It might take four inches of water to soak the soil to two feet.

During cool, overcast, still weather, about half that much water should suffice.

This can only be a rough guide. Type of plant, weather conditions, soil structure all enter into determining the amount of water needed. Since these conditions vary from place to place, you must learn from experience how much water your garden needs.

Remember that the soil should always have enough water so that plants can easily take it up into their tissues. But too much water is wasteful and leads to leaching out of precious plant foods.

The irrigation system you need depends on garden size and type of water supply. With a small garden and city water or a pressure system, a garden hose is enough. Just lay it in the bed with the end in a can or clay pot to break the flow. Do not try to irrigate by holding a hose in your hand. Your patience will run out before the garden is watered. Lay the hose down and do something else while the bed is being soaked. Try pulling weeds, for instance. They are easy to remove from wet ground.

For a big garden, without a pressurized system, be sure to choose a hose large enough to irrigate at least 25 feet of bed at a time. If the flow is too slow, the water will disappear in a few feet and you will have to move the hose too often.

We pump from a well to a reservoir about 20 feet above the garden from where water flows to the beds. Several standpipes spaced through the garden allow us to irrigate with short runs of one-inch polyethylene pipe. With this size sufficient water flows to soak 25 feet at a time. Five-eighth-inch garden hose is too small and 1¼ inch lets water out too fast. The only disadvantage of the one-inch plastic pipe is that it is easily crimped when bent.

WEEDING

Of all garden activities, weeding is the most disliked and the most neglected. But if not done regularly the vegetables will suffer, for weeds rob them of light, water, and nutrients. And their seeds will germinate to plague you year after year. And if this is not enough trouble already, weeds serve as hosts for several destructive insects and diseases.

But weeds are not all bad. Some, like mallow, lamb's-quarters, and sweet clover, are deep-rooted, bringing up nutrients from the subsoil which are deposited in the upper layers of the soil when the plants die and decay. The more shallow-rooted vegetables can utilize them. Many weeds are edible, including the young shoots of that notorious plant, the Russian thistle, which later becomes the typical tumbleweed of the Southwest. The young leaves of lamb's-quarters are a real delicacy, either eaten raw or quick-fried in oil. Purslane, a low growing succulent, is delicious, either fresh or cooked.

Unplanted garden areas should have a weed cover, especially during the rainy season. Our summer downpours can quickly remove the topsoil from unprotected earth. A weed patch need not look messy when trimmed with a sickle and edged by a wide strip of dirt.

Some weeds can be left to grow right in the bed since they do not compete strongly for water, nutrients, or light. Sweet clover, for instance, can be allowed

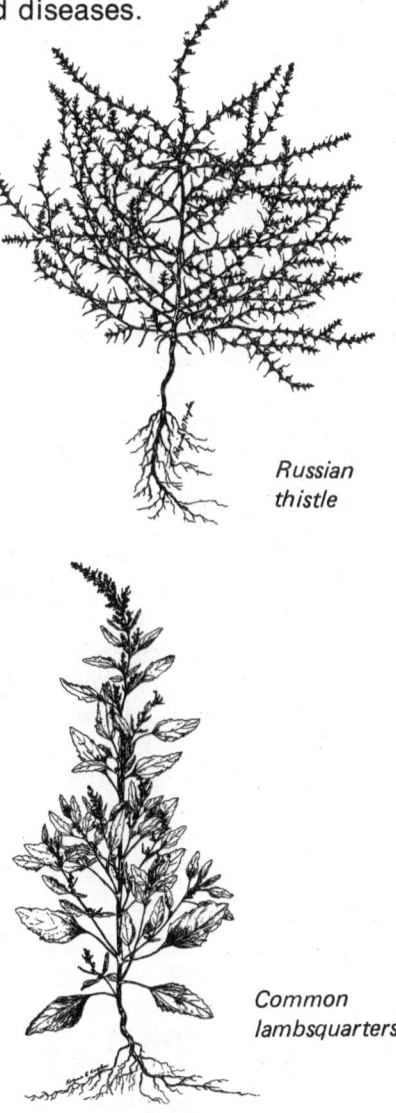

Russian thistle

Common lambsquarters

to grow among shallow-rooted plants such as onions and strawberries. Its roots go deep and its foliage is thin, so it does not compete for food and water and light. In fact, the light shade it produces probably benefits those plants, on hot, clear days when there is an over-abundance of sunshine. Purslane forms a dense carpet that cools the earth and keeps it from eroding. Since it grows low, it does not shade the vegetables.

Good weeds to be left in unused parts of the garden are sweet clover, mallow and lamb's-quarters. Being a legume, sweet clover adds nitrogen to the soil. Lamb's-quarters is deep-rooted and brings nutrients to the surface. Mallow, besides being deep-rooted, also forms a dense protective cover over the ground.

Some weeds should be eradicated wherever they are found. Russian thistle, if allowed to grow, becomes the typical tumbleweed, spreading its seeds as it rolls along. Pigweed, or amaranthus, though edible when young, forms a thorny seed when mature that pricks the hands and bare feet. Both harbor injurious insects during the winter.

The greatest need for weeding occurs at two distinct times, early in the spring and after the rainy season has begun. The early weeds are the perennial ones, like mallow, which have wintered over and are beginning to grow as the soil and air gradually warm up. They must be care-

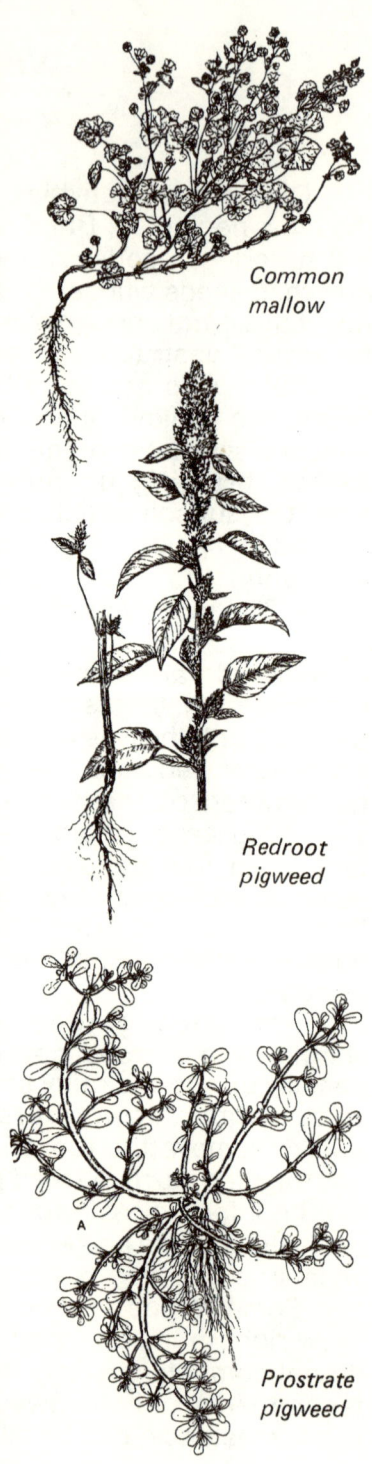

Common mallow

Redroot pigweed

Prostrate pigweed

fully removed so that they do not sprout again later. The best method is to pull them out, root and all. A simpler way is to cut through their roots several inches below the surface. This way you will be certain to remove any buds that could resprout later. But the remains of the roots could interfere when the beds are cultivated.

Common purslane

Weeding must be done again after the first heavy rains of July. Then warm weather annuals, like lamb's-quarters, pigweed and purslane, germinate, and the garden is carpeted with young weeds. Ridding the garden of them seems an impossible task, but just after they sprout it is not difficult. The plants are still small and, with the soil still damp, they are easy to remove. Just plunge the well-sharpened hoe an inch or two into the ground, and pull towards you with a scraping motion so that the weeds are thoroughly uprooted. Or use the flat-nosed shovel, again well-sharpened, and scrape under the surface. Work parallel to the bed ridges. Weeding at right angles tends to level them.

Weeds close to the vegetables must be pulled by hand. Tuck weeds in next to the vegetables to serve as a mulch. Or throw them on the compost heap, where, if still green, they will decompose fast.

Try to get all the weeds. Any left grow amazingly fast because you have removed so many of their competitors. Weed on sunny days so that the roots will dry out and die.

Weeding is more a shallow scraping than a major soil conditioning. If you dig too deeply, vegetable roots might be damaged. Ridges between beds, when cultivated too deeply, will wash away in the next heavy rains. Studies have shown that plants grow better when weeds are removed with little stirring of the soil. So restrain yourself and save your energy for the other garden work that always needs to be done.

If the spring and early summer weedings have been done conscientiously, you should have to chop out only an occasional plant the rest of the season, and the following year there should be fewer weeds. But don't expect a miracle to occur and the next garden to be weedless. Most weed seeds are long-lived and will continue to germinate for several years. Eventually, however, you should notice a marked decrease in the work needed to weed the garden.

PESTS

The organic gardener must be willing to accept some insect damage. The "perfect" fruit or vegetable he sees in the supermarket has been heavily sprayed. Without insecticides, some damage will occur, but it is better to have blemished vegetables, than ones contaminated with pesticide residues.

When a wave of insects hits your garden, do not panic and spray with pesticides. It is a self-defeating action because insecticides destroy not only harmful insects but also their enemies. Kill off the latter and you are dependent on pesticides for insect control from then on.

Do not get too discouraged when insects attack your plants. Most insects are self-limiting. Damage is limited both by their own life cycles and by their predators.

The first step to effective control is to keep every thing as natural as possible. In nature, insects are in balance with plants. It is true that garden plants are usually introduced, or exotic varieties not native to your area. But they often have wild relatives that survive. They can also, if given a chance.

Encourage rapid growth so that plants will outgrow the attacks of their pests. Sufficient water and fertilizer and regular weeding will do as much as anything to defend plants against insects. If a plant thrives in cool soil, grow it in a cool location and mulch heavily. If it prefers heat, plant it on a south slope and keep the ground bare so that it heats up.

Late planting is a simple but effective way to avoid damage. For instance, by planting after July 1, you can usually avoid most flea beetle damage.

Encourage natural predators. Build bird houses for purple martins and wrens. Birds can eat half their body weight in insects a day. Buy lady bugs and praying mantises and release them in your garden if they do not already exist there.

In spite of all these measures, plants will still need direct help. Handpicking insects, when they first appear, can destroy them before they lay their eggs and thus prevent them from multiplying. Check plants every day until all have been eliminated.

The final control is a thorough cleanup at the end of the growing season. Insects often winter on old plants, so destroy them either by thorough composting or by burning. Burning also destroys plant disease organisms that could spread through the garden on plant refuse.

Of the mammals, the gopher is the only constant menace. Although chemical repellents and even water pumped down their runs is supposed to destroy them, the only sure control I have found is a pair of spring-loaded traps. Since gophers are smart animals, the traps must be carefully placed and covered. Otherwise they will simply push dirt over the traps and jam them.

To trap gophers, find a mound of dirt they have recently pushed up. It will look fresh and moist compared to the surrounding ground. With a shovel or large trowel, dig into the mound to locate the run, which is usually from six to twelve inches down and runs in both directions. Insert two traps in the run so that the animal will be caught regardless of the direction from which he comes. Attach a small chain to each trap and bring it out of the hole and around a long stick to keep a wounded animal from dragging the traps away. Place a board over the hole and cover carefully with dirt so that no light gets through. If a gopher sees light, he will push up dirt to cover the hole and the traps will be clogged.

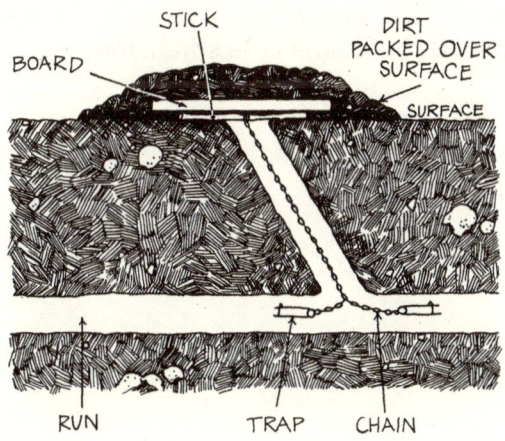

Wait a day and open the hole. If you did a careful job of covering it, you should find a dead gopher. If not, and the hole is filled with fresh dirt, dig it out and try again. Usually only one gopher lives in a run so there should be no more activity once he is trapped. Give the dead animal to your cat or dog. He will appreciate it.

Another method of general insect control, which takes little effort and brings color and variety to the garden, is the use of flowers reputed to have insect-repelling properties. We have no proof that flowers have reduced insect damage in our garden, but we have enjoyed their presence anyway.

The old-fashioned cosmos with single flowers is easy to grow, does well in our climate and makes a brilliant display of large flowers. Start a flat of cosmos about two months before the last frost. Make the drills ¼-inch deep and two inches apart. Thin the seedlings to two inches when they have their true leaves. Transplant small groups of cosmos throughout the garden, about five plants per group for maximum show. Pick off the faded blossoms and seed heads every few days and the plants will continue to bloom throughout the growing season. They can be planted in the beds with most vegetables, but beds fertilized for cabbage and related plants are too rich and the cosmos will die. Use no more than one inch of manure or sludge for this plant. Give cosmos some space since they will grow three feet tall. Once established, cosmos reseed themselves year after year, although growing them in flats will give you much earlier bloom.

The marigold is another easy-to-grow plant that is beneficial to potatoes and tomatoes. Use the odoriferous French kind, not the big American ones. Grow them in a flat like cosmos. For most effectiveness, nestle the transplants right among the plants. Since they are small, they will not crowd the vegetables.

ADVERSE WEATHER CONDITIONS

The climate of the Rocky Mountains makes gardening difficult. When we need spring rains, we have drought. As often as not, the summer rainy season never arrives, and at harvest time, we sometimes have too much rain. Though we plant as late as possible, a frost at the beginning of June blackens half our garden. Then early in September, when the garden is most beautiful, the squashes and pumpkins nearly ripe and the cucumber vines laden with fruit, a freak winter storm comes, leaving the ground covered with snow, the tender plants blackened by the cold and the squashes and pumpkins frozen. Worst of all is the heavy hailstorm which often occurs during an early summer heat wave. It leaves the ground covered with ice, and the garden smells of battered onions and corn. Some plants, like the tender cucumber vines, are destroyed for good, but the lettuce plants, though reduced to a pulpy mass, will come back, and the shredded corn still produces a crop as though nothing had happened.

Experiencing these disasters has a profound effect on our attitude toward nature. One damaging frost or hailstorm we can brush off as an abnormality, a freak deviation from nature's usual harmony with man, but when they recur, we come to the humbling conclusion that nature is completely indifferent to our aims.

Though we cannot completely escape nature's destructiveness, we can lessen the damage to our garden by becoming aware of the signs of impending disaster. Learn the average frost dates for your locale. In the mountains they can vary a great deal from place to place. For instance, on a cool still clear morning, the temperature in our garden just a few hundred feet below our house can be five degrees lower. That difference makes the growing season about two weeks shorter in the garden.

Frosts can be anticipated by watching the weather carefully in the spring or early fall, especially after a cold, winter-type storm. If the sky clears by nightfall and the air is still, a frost is likely. Cover the tender plants, the beans, squashes, cucumbers, with any cover available—boards, plastic, old clothes, mulch. Just a thin sheet of plastic will protect them from several degrees of frost.

You can have advance warning of damaging hail, too.

Look for a very tall dark thunderhead that has taken several hours to form. At our farm it usually takes shape over Hermit's Peak to the north and then moves rapidly south over us. Sometimes you can actually see a white band of hail dropping out of the cloud.

When such a storm is forming, cover everything you can with boards or heavy fabric such as blankets or rugs. Cover the whole garden if it is small and if you have enough material. Start with the most susceptible plants, the cucumbers and squashes, the lettuces, onions and beans. Some plants, such as carrots and asparagus, are never damaged and can be left uncovered.

SELLING PRODUCE

A successful commercial garden requires considerable foresight. What do people in your locality like to eat, how much will they buy, what can you grow that is superior to what is in the market now? If you do not answer these questions prior to planting, you might end up with a bountiful but unsaleable harvest.

Identifying the need comes with experience. Find out what vegetables are shipped from distant sources. If they can be grown in your climate, then you should be able to supply a cheaper and fresher product. If local truck gardens supply most of the produce consumed locally, a market for organic vegetables might exist at natural food stores or roadside stands. Talk to the county agricultural agent. He will know what is grown commercially in your area.

The situation in our region, which is typical of the Rocky Mountain region, is that almost all produce is trucked in from great distances, varying from three hundred to a thousand miles. Almost nothing is grown commercially closeby.

But this situation should soon change. Transportation costs have increased sharply, and imported produce is much more expensive than it used to be. The time is ripe for the local grower to break into the market with his freshly harvested product.

Once the need is established, the next step is to find markets for your produce. Most satisying and profitable is selling direct to the consumer. You get the full retail price for your vegetables and you have direct feedback from the buyer. If sales are bad, you cannot blame them on a poor display in the store.

The best form of direct sale is the farmers market. The consumer must come directly to you to buy, and sales are stimulated by other growers in adjacent stalls. The spirit is open and free. The buyer can concentrate on the product itself and not be distracted by glamorous packaging and mood music. The buyers sense their freedom, and vigorous bargaining results.

If a farmers' market does not exist in your area, organize one with fellow growers. Sellers need not have large amounts to sell. Variety is as important as quantity. A farmers market will succeed if consumers are offered a wide variety of high-quality vegetables.

Besides the farmers market, door-to-door sales offer the grower direct contact with buyers. Try to get advance orders so that you do not have to make many unnecessary stops. Usually the customer will refer you to neighbors so that sales rapidly build up.

If you must sell to stores or restaurants, expect to make a lot less money, because you are selling wholesale. Take a sample of your vegetables to the manager. Make sure that they are fresh, clean, and stripped of dead, unsightly leaves. Deliver your produce early in the morning before it is wilted by the sun.

Once having determined the need, you are ready to plan your commercial planting. Choose vegetables which will bring you the greatest income for the amount of space and effort they require.

Fresh sweet corn is in great demand in our area since what is sold in the supermarkets is shipped from distant farms and is starchy and flavorless. Sweet corn is at its best immediately after being picked, and what the stores offer for sale might be several weeks old. Sweet corn takes a lot of space, but it is easy to grow and harvest for sale.

Fresh peas are also easy to sell since, like corn, they are highly perishable, and are rarely seen in most stores in our region. Unlike corn, however, they take a lot of time to harvest for the income they produce.

If there are high quality restaurants or gourmet grocery stores nearby, you have an opportunity to supply them with specialty crops like shallots, which bring a high price, or with delicacies such as butter lettuce or fresh peas.

Once you know which vegetables to grow, you should determine the amount to produce, which, in turn, depends on your estimate of the market. Be sure to stagger plantings of lettuce so they do not all mature at the same time. Otherwise you might be left with beds of lettuce rapidly going to seed.

Much of the appeal of your produce will be its freshness, so on market day be prepared to rise before dawn for the harvest.

Make no compromise with quality. Only sell the best. Your reputation depends on it. No old lettuce, overripe peas, starchy corn, or deformed carrots should be taken to market. Eat them yourself.

The price to charge is sometimes hard to arrive at, because most of the value of the crop is in the labor. But try to charge a little less than the supermarket since your costs should be lower. But freshness and organic culture add to the value, so do not undervalue your vegetables. Customers are willing to pay for these features.

CULTURE OF SPECIFIC CROPS

ASPARAGUS

Introduction–Start asparagus right and have bountiful harvests for up to 20 years. For the quickest results purchase plants one year or older, but, if patient, you can easily grow ten dollars' worth of plants from a 50 cent packet of seed and only have an extra year to wait for the first harvest.

When to Plant–If you buy plants, you can set them out as soon as the soil is dry enough to work in the spring. Seeds should be started in flats about the middle of March. They will be ready for transplanting about the first of June.

What to Plant–Mary and Martha Washington are the most common varieties. They are excellent, rust-resistant types.

Where to Plant–Choose a spot with deep soil and sheltered from the prevailing wind which could bend the tender stalks.

Soil Preparation–If the top soil is thin, dig out two feet of dirt and fill with top soil enriched with four inches of manure or sludge. With better soil, it is sufficient to incorporate four inches of manure or sludge supplemented with ten pounds of wood ashes per 50 feet of bed. Prepare a wide bed and rake it smooth before planting.

Planting and Transplanting–Soak seeds over night to soften their hard coats. In a flat make half-inch drills two inches apart. Sow the seed thickly in the drills; pull dirt over the seeds; water in and cover with plastic. Asparagus seeds need heat to germinate, so set the flat in a warm place. Lift the plastic occasionally to check on soil dampness. In about three weeks, when the seeds germinate, remove the plastic. When the plants are an inch tall, thin to two inches. When three inches, transplant to the prepared garden bed. Be sure to block out the flat two weeks before transplanting. Every eighteen inches dig a hole large enough to hold the transplants. Set them in place, pack dirt around them, and water in. Purchased plants will come bare root. Build a cone of dirt in each hole and spread the roots of the plants over it so that the crown is an inch below the surface. Pack dirt around the roots with your fingers, water and mulch deeply.

Some gardening books recommend setting three-inch seedlings nine inches apart the first year and retransplanting them to 18 inches the next, but this practice sets them back. It is easiest and best to put them in their permanent places when first transplanted.

Culture of Growing Plants–Water every week until the plants are growing well. Then irrigate deeply every two weeks if the rain is inadequate. Keep plants heavily mulched to conserve moisture.

Harvest and Cleanup–Do not harvest any shoots from plants grown from seed for three years. If you start with purchased plants, you need wait only two years. The first harvest should be a small one from only the most vigorous plants and for only three weeks. The following year a full harvest of thick shoots can be made. Cut the thick stalks just below ground level before they start to branch out. Let the thin stalks grow to feed the roots for next year's crop.

In the fall, when the tops have died back, break them down and cover with two inches of manure or sludge and wood ashes at the rate of five pounds per 50-foot bed.

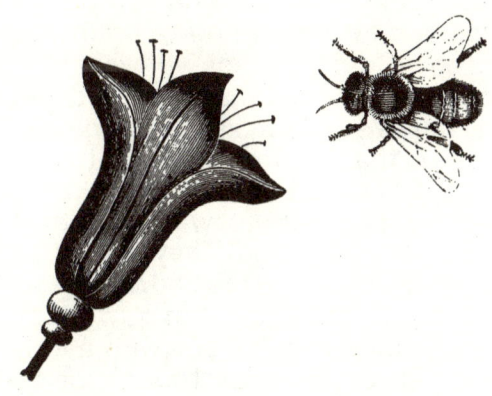

GREEN BEANS

Introduction–Beans are easy to grow and yield a good crop if watered well and harvested regularly. Fifty feet of beans will provide plenty for eating fresh and freezing, canning, or pickling.

When to Plant–Beans are tender to frost and need warm soil to grow in. Wait until about May 20 to plant, so they will miss the last frost.

Where to Plant–Plant where no beans have grown for three years.

What to Plant–Our favorite is the Blue Lake pole bean because it has a smooth cylindrical pod just right for pickling. If the Mexican bean beetle is really troublesome, plant an early bush bean that you can harvest before the beetles become pests. Otherwise pole beans are superior to the bush varieties. They yield more over a longer period of time and take up less space in the garden.

Soil Preparation–Prepare a narrow bed with one inch of manure, or sludge fortified with five pounds of wood ashes, per 50 feet of bed. Coat the seeds with vegetable oil and shake them in a can with commercial bean and pea inoculant, or with a trowel full of soil from an old bean bed. The inoculant contains bacteria that fix atmospheric nitrogen in a form that beans can use. Fork the bed and rake it smooth.

Use nine-foot poles about two inches thick and set them 18 inches deep in the ground. They should be spaced three feet apart down the center of the bed. If your soil crusts badly, spread three inches of compost in a two-foot circle around each pole and work it into the soil with a fork. This practice allows the bean sprout to break through the surface. Another way to achieve the same result is to mulch heavily once the beans are planted, but this slows down germination in cool weather. Pull the mulch aside as soon as the seeds have germinated.

Planting–Plant a circle of nine beans an inch deep and about six inches from the pole. Thick planting will make up for losses to insects and rodents. The seeds should germinate in ten days.

Culture of Growing Plants–After the seedlings are about four inches high, thin all but the three or four strongest plants. As the vines grow, wind any sprawling runners around the poles so that they will grow upwards.

Pests–The only serious pest is the Mexican bean beetle, which is shaped like a lady bug but is larger and brown instead of orange. It should be destroyed immediately, for, if unchecked, it will make skeletons of the vines. Also look for the larvae and pupae, which are orange, spiny creatures. All forms of this troublesome insect, including the orange eggs, are found on the underside of leaves.

Harvest and Cleanup–Pick beans continuously to prolong the harvest. Near the end of the season, let some of them mature and dry. Shell the beans and keep the seed for next year. Do not keep seed for longer than one year. Old seed is difficult to germinate because the seed coat is too hard. Pull the old vines and destroy by burning to keep them from spreading diseases.

BEETS

Introduction –Beets do well in our cool climate. Their fresh greens are good raw in salads and cooked in soups. The roots can be stored for winter use or canned and pickled.

When to Plant –Beets are hardy and can be planted from May until 60 days before the first fall frost. If you plan to make only one planting, wait until July 1 and take advantage of the summer rains.

Where to Plant –Beets prefer a cool location, if grown during the hot part of the summer. Plant where no beets or chard have grown for three years.

What to Plant –We grow the Detroit Dark Red variety, which matures in about 60 days and allows us to make a July 1 planting.

Soil Preparation –Prepare a wide bed with one inch of manure or sludge supplemented with five pounds of wood ashes per 50-foot bed. Fork and rake smooth.

Planting –Dig two half-inch drills a foot apart in the bed. Sow one seed per inch, cover, and keep the rows moist until the seedlings appear, in a week to ten days. Seedlings can be transplanted with a fair degree of success if you need to fill in blank spaces in the row. Carefully dig out excess plants with a trowel, preserving as many of the roots as possible. Set the plants in their places with the tap root pointed down. Pack dirt around the plants and water in. In dry weather, water every day for a week. If you soak the seeds overnight, they will germinate faster and more evenly.

Culture of Growing Plants –Since beet seeds are really fruits with several seeds, they will send up several shoots from each fruit. All but one should be pulled.

Thin to two inches when the plants are two inches tall. When roots are two inches in diameter, thin to four inches. Small beets are tender and delicious.

Give beets about an inch of water a week. This will keep moisture around the roots. Mulching helps preserve a moist environment.

Harvest, Storage, and Cleanup –Beets can take frost but should be dug before the ground freezes hard. Here the date is about November 1. Store roots in a cool, damp place. Destroy the old plants by burning.

BROCCOLI

Introduction—Broccoli is a member of the cabbage family and is grown the same way. It takes a lot of room for the yield, but the taste of broccoli picked at its prime is worth the space it needs.

When to Plant—Broccoli is tough and coarse when grown in hot weather, so wait until the rainy season to grow it. Late planting also avoids the flea beetle.

Where to Plant—Broccoli demands a cool location, like a north slope.

What to Plant—Green Comet, an early hybrid, is available from Gurney's. It will mature even when planted as late as July 1.

Soil Preparation—See cabbage.
Planting and Transplanting—See cabbage.
Culture of Growing Plants—See cabbage.
Pests—See cabbage.

Harvest and Cleanup—Pick the flower clusters when they are full-sized but before the flowers open. After the chief cluster is harvested, the plant will produce many smaller clusters. Plants should be checked daily since the flowers open quickly. When heavy frost threatens, cover the plants at night. During the fall they will continue to yield but in smaller amounts.

When the season is finally over, pull the plants and feed them to your chickens or goats. Burn the main stems to destroy any flea beetle eggs.

BRUSSELS SPROUTS

Introduction – Brussels sprouts are a member of the cabbage group and are grown in the same way. They are very hardy and will bear until Thanksgiving without protection.

When to Plant – Since Brussels sprouts take about three months to mature, they should be transplanted by June 1. Start plants on April 1.

Where to Plant – Brussels sprouts need a cool situation.

What to Plant – Long Island Improved is one of the dwarf varieties which yields relatively early.

Soil Preparation – See cabbage.

Planting and Transplanting – See cabbage.

Culture of Growing Plants – See cabbage.

Pests – The grey cabbage aphid attacks the sprouts themselves. Crush the insects as best you can.

Harvest and Cleanup – Pick the sprouts when they are an inch to an inch-and-a-half in diameter. Remove leaves from around the harvested sprouts and give them to the animals. Each plant yields about a quart of sprouts.

CABBAGE

Introduction–Cabbage is an ideal plant for our climate if it survives the onslaughts of the flea beetle and harlequin bug.

When to Plant–To escape the flea beetle and to take advantage of the cool temperatures of the rainy season, cabbage plants should go into the garden around July 1. This means that flats must be started about May 15.

Where to Plant–Cabbage needs a cool location.

What to Plant–Choose one of the so-called second early cabbages. We use Red Acre and Marion Market. Both make good-sized heads which store well.

Soil Preparation–Cabbage is a heavy feeder, and you will be rewarded with bigger heads if you use a lot of manure. Prepare a narrow bed with four inches of manure or sludge. With the latter spread ten pounds of wood ashes per 50 feet of bed. Fork the bed and rake it smooth.

Planting and Transplanting–Obtain potting soil for your cabbage flat away from the garden so that it will not contain flea beetles or their eggs. Make drills about two inches apart and a quarter-inch deep. Sprinkle the seeds in the drills and pull soil over them. Water and cover the flat with plastic. When the seedlings emerge (about four days later), remove the plastic and place the flat in the cold frame. The seedlings should grow rapidly. If they don't, sprinkle about one-half inch of manure around the plants and they will perk up. When the weather is hot and dry, cabbage seedlings and related plants do better when they are partially shielded from the sun. Cover the flat with window screen or cheese cloth. Thin cabbages to stand two inches apart. Around June 15, block out the plants with a spatula. Two weeks later, transplant to the garden, spacing plants 18 inches apart in the row. If you grow a small variety like Golden Acre, 12 inches apart is sufficient. The largest types require two feet. Water in as soon as transplanted, and cover plants if they wilt in the midday sun. The plants will look somewhat limp for a couple of weeks, but then they will start to grow.

Culture of Growing Plants–Once established, cabbages do well with a weekly watering, but for the first two weeks after transplanting they need frequent individual watering, especially if the weather is hot, dry, or windy. Mulching between plants will help conserve moisture and keep the soil cool until the plants have grown large enough to shade the ground.

***Pests**—*Keep a close watch for injurious insects. The harlequin bug, a bright orange and black insect with a shield-shaped back, about half-an-inch long, appears usually in the middle of July. Uncontrolled it can destroy a planting, but daily handpicking will curb its damage. Also check for yellow egg cases under the plant leaves.

More destructive and harder to control is the flea beetle, a tiny black insect that has an inexhaustible appetite for members of the cabbage family. Fortunately it becomes much less numerous after July 1, so by late planting we escape a lot of flea beetle damage.

If you insist, however, on growing cabbages or related plants early in season, you can subdue if not eliminate the flea beetle by trapping them on sticky boards. Coat two foot-square pieces of cardboard with a thin layer of honey, molasses or other sticky substance. Place on the ground against the stem of each plant and gently shake. Many of the beetles will jump to the boards and be trapped. When finished with the row, rub the pieces together to crush the insects. This may have to be done twice a day when beetle infestations are heavy.

The cabbage looper, a green worm which humps its back when moving, sometimes damages young cabbage plants by eating large holes in the leaves. Check the underside of the leaves each day until the worms have been destroyed.

Harvest, Storage, and Cleanup—As soon as cabbages reach full-size, they should be picked and stored. If allowed to stand in the garden after maturity, they will start cracking. Pull out the plants and cut off the roots. Break off the loose outer leaves. They make excellent green feed for poultry and goats. Do not remove the tight but ragged head leaves. They serve as a protective cover. Store the heads either in a root cellar or pile them outside, covered with a couple of feet of straw or weeds. Do not keep them in the house or near apples. The strong pervasive odor is absorbed by the fruit. Stored cabbages will keep their good flavor until March.

CARROTS

Introduction–Carrots thrive in our climate and soil, store well in the ground through the winter, and make a good food for chickens when greens are in short supply. They are hard to germinate, but once up they are easy to grow.

When to Plant–In our climate, carrots can be planted from May 1 to July 1. The early plantings will provide you with carrots late in the summer, but they take more effort to grow because the seeds need frequent sprinklings to germinate in the dry, hot part of the growing season. A July 1 planting coincides with the beginning of the rainy season; with luck almost no hand watering will be needed, and you will have better germination than with earlier plantings.

Where to Plant–Choose a spot with the sandiest soil.

What to Plant–In our heavy soils, it is unwise to plant the long, thin carrot which you find in the supermarket. It is grown in sandy soil, saturated with fertilizer. But in heavier soils it only makes a thin, mishapen root, unless you add at least three or four inches of sand. Except for a tiny planting, adding that much sand is not worth the effort since you can grow shorter and fatter varieties that taste just as good and require much less soil preparation.

If your soil is heavy clay, grow the Oxheart variety (also called Guermande). It is only four inches long, and often just as thick. Hence only four inches of soil need to be improved. Two inches of sand or three inches of compost will make the heaviest of clay soils fit for growing this variety.

With an average soil like ours a medium length carrot can be grown with the addition of just one inch of goat or cow manure. We usually grow either the cone-shaped Chantenay or the cylindrical Nantes. They taste about the same and are equally easy to grow, though the thicker Chantenay is less likely to break when dug out of frozen or dry ground.

Soil Preparation–Since carrot seed is small and the seedlings fragile, the seed bed must be carefully prepared. First spread one inch of well-rotted, pulverized manure on the wide bed and then add ten pounds of wood ashes per 50 feet of bed. Fork the bed and break the clumps. Rake with extra care, going back and forth until the top several inches are free of lumps over one-half inch in diameter. If larger pieces are left, they could keep seedlings from breaking through the surface.

Planting–Carrots can be planted either as a solid bed or in rows. The former method insures that the plants will eventually form a continuous cover over the bed. The latter puts the seeds in marked lines where they are easier to water and weed.

If you follow the first method, sprinkle the seeds as uniformly as possible over the whole bed. Be generous with the seeds. Carrots do not germinate well even under the best of conditions. An average of one carrot seed every quarter inch should be enough to insure a solid stand.

Next, sprinkle a half inch of fine, moist compost evenly over the bed. If the compost is clumpy, put it through a one-half inch mesh screen. Hardware cloth is the best. Dry compost should be soaked with water and massaged with the hands until uniformly moist. Then apply it to the bed. If you try to moisten compost after it is in place, water will pass right through, leaving the compost dry.

After the seeds are covered, water the bed with a watering can or with a hose. Set the nozzle to give a fine spray. A solid stream of water might wash out the seeds.

Cover the bed with mulch, pine needles, plastic, rags, cardboard, whatever is available. Sprinkle the planting every other day, especially during periods of dry weather. Make sure the water goes through the mulch into the ground. When the carrots start to come up, in about ten days, remove the mulch and continue watering until you have a solid planting.

To sow carrots in rows, place two stakes about a foot apart at each end of the bed. Then using the stakes as a guide, make half inch drills with a hoe. They should be about two inches wide and rectangular in cross section. Sow seeds generously in the wide drills and cover with one-half inch of moist sifted compost and water in. Proceed from here as with the solid bed method.

Be sure to remove the mulch as soon as the carrots emerge. Otherwise they will be leggy and weak.

Culture of Growing Plants—Once the seeds are up, you are past the hardest part of growing carrots. As long as they receive sufficient water and timely thinnings and weedings, they will take care of themselves.

At first, give the planting about one inch of water a week. When the rainy season starts, you should not have to water again until early fall.

Thin the seedlings to half an inch apart when they have their true leaves. The final thinning should be done when young carrots are about a half inch in diameter. Thin the

Nantes variety to 1½ inches, the Chantenay to two and the Oxheart to three. The thinnings are delicious.

Pests–The yellow carrot caterpillar, a yellow insect as pretty as its name, usually causes little damage but if you grow lots of carrots, it may become a nuisance. The young insects are darker than at maturity.

Harvest and Storage–From the time they are a half inch thick, carrots can be harvested. But for the biggest yield, wait until they reach their full size. They won't be as tender, but they will be sweeter.

Because of our moderate climate, carrots can be safely left in the ground through the winter. When the heavy frosts come almost every night, cover the bed with a deep layer of mulch. It will keep the ground from freezing for a month or more of late fall weather. If you dig carrots before the ground freezes solid, store them in a cool, damp place in damp sand. Cut off all but a half inch of the tops. Tops draw water from the roots and make them shrivel.

Sometimes in December and January, the ground will freeze too hard to dig. Then you will have to wait until there have been several days of 50 degree weather. Such warm spells occur regularly here in the southern Rockies, even in the depth of winter. After such a thaw, uncover the bed in the morning when the temperature reaches 32 degrees. By three in the afternoon the ground should be soft enough to dig. Harvest a lot at once. They may have to last a couple of weeks until the next thaw.

CAULIFLOWER

Introduction – Cauliflower, a member of the cabbage family, takes more care to raise than the average garden vegetable, but the taste of the fresh, home-grown product is worth the extra effort.

When to Plant – Start your plants indoors about April 15 and transplant around May 15.

Where to Plant – Choose a cool location for cauliflower.

What to Plant – Choose one of the early varieties like Snowball Y available from Burrell's. Purple Head, though not listed as an early variety, does well in our short growing season and has a more subtle flavor than the white varieties.

Soil Preparation – Cauliflower demands a rich soil. Cover a narrow bed with four inches of manure or sludge (fortified with ten pounds of wood ashes per 50 feet of bed). Fork in the fertilizer and rake smooth.

Planting and Transplanting – If you are growing only a few plants, start them in small cups or cans. Otherwise use a flat. See the cabbage article for details.

Transplant about the middle of May. If you used a flat, block out the seedlings around the first of May. Dig small holes with trowel every 18 inches, set in the transplants, and firm the soil around them. Water in and cover those plants which wilt during the heat of the day. A number 2½ can with one end removed and the other barely attached makes a convenient cover. It can be pushed down when the plant wilts or if a hail storm threatens.

Culture of Growing Plants – Give cauliflower an inch of water a week. Mulch thickly to conserve moisture and cool the soil. Side dress with a cup of chicken manure around each plant when the heads begin to form, to increase their size.

Just before the heads mature (when they are still compact and do not yet look grainy), they should be covered to blanch them and make them sweet. Leaves can be broken off and laid over the heads, but a better way is to tuck a sheet of newspaper around the head and leave it in place for a couple of days. Be sure to remove it before the florets separate. If you're too late, the heads will be less attractive, but they will be still edible.

Pests – See cabbage.

Harvest, Storage, and Cleanup – Pick cauliflower before the florets open. Cauliflower is a treat either fresh, frozen, or pickled.

Feed the leaves to your live stock and burn the stalks which may harbor flea beetles.

CELERIAC

Introduction – Though less demanding about climate and soil than celery, celeriac (or celery root) is still more trouble to grow than most vegetables. But it provides a unique flavoring for soups, or a delicious side dish when cooked and then marinated in oil and vinegar.

What to Plant – Celeriac is available from Gurney's and DeGiorgi.

Where to Plant – Plant in a cool, damp location. Next to a hose bibb is ideal.

When to Plant – Start seed in flats about ten weeks before transplanting time. We begin ours about the middle of March.

Soil Preparation – Celeriac must have a rich soil. Apply two inches of manure or sludge with ten pounds of wood ashes per 50 feet of bed. Fork in the fertilizer and break up the clumps.

Planting and Transplanting – Because of the way they must be raised, celeriac seedlings are very susceptible to damping off. To control this disease, sterilize the soil in the flat by twice pouring boiling water through it. At the same time sterilize a can of finely sifted soil to cover the seeds with. Wait a day for the soil to become workable and then plant. Sprinkle seeds in drills a half inch deep and two inches apart. Cover with sifted soil from the can, water thoroughly, and cover with plastic. The seeds should germinate within ten days.

Keep seedlings in the shade for ten days and water often with a fine spray so that the top does not dry out. Then the plants can have sun, starting with 15 minutes the first day and increasing 15 minutes a day until the plants are out all day. Gradually thin to two inches in the row. Keep the plants moist at all times.

When the seedlings are four inches tall, transplant to the garden. Set six inches apart in the row.

Culture of Growing Plants – Keep heavily mulched since plants must be constantly moist. Water deeply at least once a week.

Harvest and Storage – Roots may be left in the ground until heavy frost threatens. Store roots in damp sand; they will retain their flavor for several months.

CHIVES

Introduction–Once established, chives need little care. Though they die back in the winter, they reappear every spring. Though we ignore them, they still thrive.

When to Plant–Plant seed or divisions from clumps any time during the growing season.

Where to Plant–Plant throughout the garden. Their smell will help repel insects.

What to Plant–You should be able to find a friend with an extra clump of plants. Otherwise, buy the seeds on a seed rack.

Soil Preparation–Chives thrive on rich soil. See the section on onions.

Planting and Transplanting–Sow the seed one-quarter inch deep and keep moist. Plant among other vegetables to repel insects.

Culture of Growing Plants–Chives can be ignored and they will still thrive. But during prolonged droughts, they should be watered. After about three years when the clumps become crowded, they should be divided and replanted.

Harvest–Young shoots are sweeter than the older ones. In late fall, pot a small clump for indoor use during the winter. Chives left in the garden will die back but will reappear early in the spring.

SWEET CORN

Introduction – Without exaggeration, sweet corn is a miracle plant. In spite of adverse weather, cold nights, cool days, and heavy hail, corn always makes a good crop. I have seen our one-quarter acre of corn transformed by hail from a sea of green leaves to a wretched field of stalks which look like green mops stuck upside down in the ground. And yet those plants go on to produce a heavy crop.

When to Plant – Plant seed at weekly intervals so that you will have corn ripening for several weeks. Since the average date for the last frost here is May 20, we make our first planting on May 15. If we lose it to a late frost, we can always replant. We make two more plantings, on the 22nd and the 29th of May.

Where to Plant – Give corn a warm location. A south slope is ideal.

What to Plant – The key to success is to choose the right variety for the climate. Full-season types like Illini Chief will not mature here. They need a long, hot growing season. Of the successful early varieties New Sunburst (also called Sunburst Improved) is the best we have tried. It makes a long, full ear which stays at the right state of ripeness for several weeks. The husks extend over the tip of the ear and are tightly closed, which discourages the ear worm. New Sunburst can be obtained from Gurney's, Midwest, Burrell's, and Rocky Mountain seed companies.

Soil Preparation – Because corn seed is large and vigorous, the soil does not need as much preparation as with smaller seeds, but all large clumps should definitely be broken up. By planting corn in a single row, you need only prepare a narrow bed. Spread two inches of manure or sludge with five pounds of wood ashes per 50 feet of bed. Fork in the fertilizer and rake the bed smooth.

Planting – If the bed is dry, water it about two days before planting. With the shovel attachment on the wheel hoe or with a hand hoe, make a drill about two inches deep down the middle of the bed. Drop seeds about three or four inches apart in the drill and immediately cover with dirt to keep the moisture in. They should germinate without additional water. As the seedlings begin to break through the surface, check for soil crusting which can prevent the plants from emerging. Break up the crust with a rake. Be gentle or you will damage the tender seedlings underneath.

Be sure to plant several rows of corn and not just one long row. Corn is cross-pollinated, and pollen must fall on the silks from adjacent plants for the ears to be completely formed.

Culture of Growing Plants–Thin the plants to six or eight inches apart when they are three inches tall. The thinnings are good goat feed. If you make a wide bed and plant two rows, thin the plants to stand one foot apart.

After one month of growth, corn roots extend only a foot into the soil, so shallow, but relatively frequent irrigations, are most suitable. During the hot, dry weather in June, watch for signs of water stress. If the leaves roll, the corn needs water immediately. When corn is two months old, bi-weekly two-inch irrigations are adequate, but by then the rains should provide most of the water needed. After the ears have formed, irrigation can be stopped.

When corn is young, it needs regular weeding, but when full-size it will shade the ground and suppress the weeds.

Pests–The only pest we have is the ear worm, which eats the end of every third or fourth ear. If you live in a hotter area with a longer growing season than ours, the ear worm can eat up a lot of the ear and make it almost inedible. The best method of control is to squirt several drops of mineral oil into the tip of the ear when the silks have started to dry up. The oil will smother the growing worm.

Raccoons, rabbits, birds, and mice all take their share of the harvest, but it rarely amounts to a sizeable portion.

Harvest, Storage, and Cleanup–When the ear is ripe, it will drop away from the stalk. The kernels should be full and yellow. When broken, they contain a milky fluid. In our cool climate, corn stays at its peak for about two weeks. If the kernels are dented and their contents doughy, the ear is past the most edible stage. Overripe ears can be dried for cornmeal or animal food. Husk the ears and leave them in a sunny place until they are completely dry. Do not bother to save the seed of hybrid corn. It will not breed true.

For maximum sweetness, eat sweet corn right after you harvest it.

When the corn is all picked, pull out the plants (or cut them off near the ground) and stack them up, tepee-style. Tie the top with bailing wire and the pile will not blow over in the wind. Feed the stalks to your livestock.

CUCUMBERS

Introduction–We have enough warmth here to raise a good crop of cucumbers, which are almost pest-free as a bonus. But they can be severely damaged by hail and are very tender to frost, so the harvest is often reduced by these conditions.

When to Plant–Since cucumbers are very tender, they should not be planted before May 20. With a short growing season, cucumbers should be started in plastic containers three weeks before the last expected frost.

Where to Plant–Cucumbers flourish on a warm, sunny slope, where frost damage is a little less likely too. Plant where neither cucumbers nor melons have grown for three years.

What to Plant–Early Russian, a pickling cucumber, available from DeGiorgi is very early and exceptionally productive. For eating fresh, both Marketer and Ashley are good choices. They have a waxy, thick skin, unlike the pickling varieties.

Soil Preparation–Cucumbers are heavy feeders and require a thick application of manure. On a narrow bed, spread four inches of manure or sludge. Fortify the sludge with ten pounds of wood ashes per 50 feet of bed. Fork in the fertilizer and rake smooth. Leave an adjacent bed vacant for the vines to run in. Prepare the bed several weeks before planting because cucumber seed could rot if it comes in contact with fresh manure or sludge.

Planting and Transplanting–With a stick make an inch hole every three inches. Drop in a seed and cover. If the soil crusts, cover with a mulch and keep moist until the seeds germinate, in about ten days to two weeks. After the seeds are up, thin to a foot apart.

If you start seeds indoors, fill small containers with potting soil and plant three or four seeds an inch deep. You can use peat pots and plant the whole container in the garden. In this way the roots will not be disturbed. But if you are careful, you can use plastic or paper containers and separate the root ball without injury. One-half pint yogurt containers make ideal pots. They can be cut open and the plants transferred to the garden without damaging them.

After the seedlings emerge in the pot, thin to the most vigorous plant. When no more frost is likely, transplant to the garden. Space the plants one foot apart and water frequently for a week, or until the roots have spread into the surrounding soil.

Culture of Growing Plants–Especially when they begin to form fruit, cucumbers need a constant supply of water. If moisture is lacking, the fruit becomes bitter. Usually fruiting time coincides with the rainy season, but if rain is lacking, irrigate promptly. Bearing plants should have two inches of water a week. Train the vines to grow into a vacant bed.

Harvest and Cleanup–Harvest pickling cucumbers when they are about three inches long. If allowed to grow larger, they will be hollow. Also remove any yellow, ripening fruit and feed them to the animals. With the vines picked clean, plants will continue to set fruit. If you grow fresh eating varieties, let them grow to their full size, but pick before they start to turn yellow. If they are bitter to the taste, they have not received enough water.

When frost comes and the vines die, pull them from the ground and destroy by burning.

GARLIC

Introduction –Garlic is similar to onions in its fertilizer needs and culture.

When to Plant –The cloves can be planted in May or June.

What to Plant –You have several kinds to choose from. Elephant garlic is a large, mild-flavored variety. The other white kind is medium-sized. The red is the smallest, but it stores best of all. Both the red and white kinds can be purchased in the supermarket. Elephant garlic must be bought from seed companies. The average bulb has about fifteen cloves.

Soil Preparation –See the section on onions.

Planting –With a hoe or wheel hoe dig two trenches a foot apart and two inches deep. Place the cloves four to six inches apart with the top of the clove pointed upwards. Cover with dirt.

Culture of Growing Plants –See the section on onions.

Harvest and Storage –When the tops have turned brown, the bulbs should be dug and dried thoroughly in the air. Bulbs need to be stored in a cool but dry place. Garlic will store well if the bulbs are divided, the cloves spread out on a plate and then kept in a closed jar. Check them occasionally for mildew. If it occurs, the cloves need further drying.

Reserve cloves from the largest bulbs for planting the next year.

HORSE BEANS

Introduction–The horse bean is also known as the broad bean or fava bean. The local Spanish name is haba. Horse beans are a traditional crop of the cooler parts of the southwestern mountains. They can be shelled green and eaten like a lima bean, or allowed to mature and cooked like other dry beans.

What to Plant–Horse beans (listed as broad beans) are available from the Rocky Mountain Seed Co. Or they can be bought from Spanish food racks in grocery stores.

When to Plant–Plant horse beans around the first of May, since they are hardy to frost.

Soil Preparation–If possible, inoculate the bed with soil in which horse beans have grown before. The dirt will contain nitrogen-fixing bacteria specific to this bean and will stimulate its growth. Then spread a half inch of manure or sludge and five pounds of wood ashes per 50-foot bed. Fork the mixture in and break up clumps with a cultivator or rake.

Planting and Transplanting–When growing a single row in the bed, plant every three inches and later thin to six. If a double row is grown, plant every six inches and thin to twelve. Push seeds one to two inches into ground. They germinate in about ten days.

Culture of Growing Plants–Horse beans are easy to grow. Just be sure to give them a good weekly or, if the weather has been cool, bi-weekly watering.

Pests–The young stems are sometimes attacked by black aphids. Remove by crushing or by blasting with a strong stream of water. Lady bugs should help clear the stems of any remaining aphids.

Harvest and Storage–When harvested green, the beans should be full size, but the pods should still be green. Wait until the pods turn black to pick the dry beans. Destroy the old plants to keep from spreading disease to other parts of the garden.

HORSE RADISH

***Introduction**-*If planted in rich soil and watered regularly, horseradish should thrive without much attention. It can be used as a trap for harlequin bugs.

***When to Plant**-*Set the roots in the ground as soon as it is dry enough to be worked in the spring.

***Where to Plant**-*Choose a cool location where no member of the cabbage family has grown for several years.

***What to Plant**-*Horseradish roots can be obtained from many seed companies.

***Soil Preparation**-*An inch of manure is sufficient for horseradish. Fork the fertilizer in and rake the bed smooth.

***Planting and Transplanting**-*Down the center of a narrow bed, dig a trench four or five inches deep and lay six to eight inch root cuttings at an angle in the trench. Space them 18 inches apart. Cover the cuttings so as not to disturb the angle of the roots. Water in.

***Culture of Growing Plants**-*Give the plant an average of one inch of water a week. A thick mulch will keep the soil cool.

***Pests**-*Flea beetles and harlequin bugs relish horseradish. Use the controls suggested in the section on cabbage. Since horseradish comes up early in the spring, it will serve as a trap for harlequin bugs before they have laid their eggs. Regularly pick off the bugs every morning and you should have fewer later in the season.

***Harvest and Storage**-*Dig the roots in the fall after they have thickened. If you leave the side shoots from the main root behind, they will come up the following spring. Or you can dig the whole plant and save the thinner side shoots for planting the next year. Store in a cool place.

KALE

Introduction—Though we find kale too strong for eating, we have grown it for animal feed.

When to Plant—Plant after July 1 to miss most of the flea beetles.

Where to Plant—Kale is related to cabbage and prefers a cool location.

What to Plant—Dwarf Green Curled yields early and well.

Soil Preparation—Like cabbage, except that you should prepare a wide bed.

Planting—Sow seeds thickly one-quarter inch deep in double rows one foot apart. Mulch and keep the bed moist until the seedlings appear. Draw the mulch back so the plants will have sufficient light.

Culture of Growing Plants—Thin plants until they stand one foot apart. Proceed cautiously; the flea beetles may do some of the thinning for you. Mulch to keep the soil cool.

Pests—See cabbage.

Harvest and Cleanup—Pick off the outer leaves from the plants, and the centers will continue to yield until late fall. If mulched well, kale will come up again in early spring before it goes to seed.

KOHLRABI

Introduction—Kohlrabi, a member of the cabbage family, is grown for its bulb-like main stem. Like broccoli, it takes up much space and yields little. Only grow it if you have plenty of garden space and a great taste for this strange vegetable.

When to Plant—See cabbage.

Where to Plant—Choose a cool location.

What to Plant—Plant either White or Purple Vienna kohlrabi.

Soil Preparation—Kohlrabi is a spreading plant. Plant in a single row in a narrow bed. See cabbage for the details of soil preparation.

Planting and Transplanting—See cabbage.

Culture of Growing Plants—See cabbage.

Pests—See cabbage.

Harvest and Cleanup—Pick when the center is two or three inches in diameter. Use the leaves for animal feed and destroy the main stem.

LETTUCE

Introduction–In our mild climate lettuce is one of the most reliable vegetables. It not only provides greens early in the spring but yields well through the summer and into the fall.

When to Plant–For the earliest greens, lettuce should be started in the cold frame. We start a flat about March 15 for setting out on May 1. For a continuous supply, make a small planting every two weeks until the middle of July. By the middle of May lettuce can be seeded directly in the garden.

Where to Plant–Lettuce needs a cool location or it will quickly go to seed in a prolonged hot spell.

What to Plant–For a variety of leaf lettuce, plant Black-seeded Simpson for the earliest heads; Grand Rapids, with its interesting curled leaf; Buttercrunch, a bibb-type that is both delicious and heat-resistant; and Parris Island Cos, a romaine type, which takes about 90 days. All four are available from many seed companies or on seed racks. I do not recommend growing head lettuce since it is difficult to raise and not as nutritious as leaf lettuce.

Soil Preparation–On a wide bed, add one inch of manure or sludge with five pounds of wood ashes per 50 feet of bed. Fork the bed and rake it smooth. If you seed directly in the bed, rake more thoroughly than when transplanting.

Planting and Transplanting–In a flat, make quarter-inch drills about two inches apart and sprinkle in the seed. Cover the drills, water in the seeds, and cover with plastic. Keep the boxes in a warm place and the seeds will germinate in about four days. When the seeds are up, immediately transfer the flats to the cold frame. Thin the plants to stand two inches apart in the row when they have their true leaves.

Two weeks before the date for transplanting, slice carefully between the plants to the bottom of the box. This will force the roots to grow in a ball and will reduce transplant shock. Set lettuce transplants with their root balls intact eight inches apart in the bed. Pack dirt around the plants to eliminate any air pockets and water thoroughly. Try to do the transplanting on a cloudy, cool day. This will lessen the shock. If the plants wilt in the midday sun, cover with pots or boxes until the heat of the day is past. Within a week the plants should be able to take the full sun without wilting.

If you do not use flats, sow seeds at one end of the bed

and transplant the thinnings into the rest of the bed. Be sure to keep the soil moist until the seedlings emerge. Daily sprinklings or a thick mulch will help. If insects or rodents eat the seedlings, you can transplant thinnings to fill the gaps. Thin to eight inches when plants are an inch high.

Culture of Growing Plants–When the plants form a continuous cover and begin to crowd each other, the harvest should start. Pick every other one and the remaining plants will have space to grow to full size. When plants are crowded, the leaves become paper thin. In hot, dry weather, lettuce needs two inches of water a week to stay in top condition. Under normal weather conditions, however, an inch a week is sufficient. Without sufficient water lettuce grows slowly, goes to seed early, and is bitter to the taste.

Harvest–Either pick the outer leaves or harvest the entire plant. When the weather turns cold in the fall, you can prolong the season for about a month by covering the plants each night when frost threatens.

MULTIPLIER ONIONS

Introduction–Once planted, multiplier onions really take care of themselves. They even replant themselves by bending over to force bulbs which have formed at the ends of the stalks into the ground.

When to Plant–This plant can be set in the garden any time in the growing season.

What to Plant–You should be able to find a neighbor with a surplus he will be happy to give away.

Soil Preparation–Like other onions, the multiplier type likes a rich soil, with the nutrients concentrated in the top foot of soil. Fork in an inch of manure or sludge and five pounds of wood ashes per 50 feet of bed. Rake the bed smooth.

Planting–Easiest to plant are the cloves which form at the tips of the plants. Press a clove into the ground so that it is just covered with dirt. Spacing is six inches each way. If cloves are unavailable, plants can be substituted. Be sure to pack dirt around the roots and water well.

Culture of Growing Plants–An inch of water every week is sufficient. In the spring or fall mulch with an inch of manure or sludge and wood ashes. Multiplier onions are self-sufficient plants.

Harvest–Simply cut off whatever you need at the moment.

ONIONS

Introduction—Our short growing season makes producing a large, completely mature onion a challenge, and sometimes we don't succeed. Sometimes the bulbs are small and the necks thick. But if you succeed, the beautiful onions you get are worth the effort.

When to Plant—Onion seeds should be started about 2½ months before transplanting time, that is, February 15, for setting out May 1. Seed must be started in flats. You can't grow mature onions if you seed directly in the garden because of the short growing season.

What to Plant—I strongly recommend that you raise your onions from seed rather than sets. Seeds are available in great variety. Onions grown from seed rarely go to seed themselves, and you get a larger proportion of bulbs with dry, thin necks. But if you choose not to raise onions from seed, buy young plants rather than sets. The yellow types store well, and the reds and whites are especially mild and good in salads.

Soil Preparation—Onions are heavy feeding, shallow-rooted plants. They need a two inch layer of rotted manure. Do not use sludge if onions are eaten raw. Fork in the manure and rake the wide bed smooth.

Planting and Transplanting—In a flat, make drills one inch apart and one-quarter inch deep. Sprinkle in the seed and cover with dirt. Wet thoroughly and keep the flat covered until the seeds germinate, in about a week. Then transfer the flat to the cold frame. Thin the plants to an inch apart when they are an inch tall.

Onion seedlings should grow rapidly to be pencil thick at transplanting time. But if they are sluggish, sprinkle the flat with a half inch of manure.

When transplanting time comes, upturn the flat, dump out the plants, and separate them. Don't worry if the dirt comes away from the roots. Onions are hardy and can take the shock. But keep the sun off the plants until they are in the ground.

With a hoe or wheel hoe, dig two four-inch deep trenches a foot apart down the bed. Lay the plants in the trench four inches apart for small varieties like Ebenezer or six inches apart for large types like Yellow Sweet Spanish. Pull soil over the plants and firm it with the hoe. Water in and keep the soil moist until the plants resume growing.

Culture of Growing Plants–A thick mulch around the plants keeps the soil moist and helps to prevent the bulbs from splitting.

Onions need a weekly one-inch watering until the bulbs are full-sized. Remove all weeds since they compete strongly when young with the shallow-rooted onions.

When bulbs reach full size, crush the tops down to speed the drying of the necks.

Harvest and Storage–Harvest in several stages. For the first picking, dig only the mature bulbs and lay them in the sun for a few hours to dry. Then cut off the necks and store. Harvest the rest of the onions before a severe frost. Bring them inside the house and spread them on the floor to dry. When the necks have shriveled and turned brown, they should be cut off and the onions stored.

Ideal storage for onions is a cool, dry place—an unheated room which does not freeze. A root cellar is too damp, and even fully ripe onions will quickly mildew. Better than a cool, damp cellar is a warm, but dry, house. Store onions loose in a well-ventilated container. Or, if you only have a few, braid the tops and hang them from the ceiling.

PARSLEY AND TURNIP-ROOTED PARSLEY

Introduction–Though trickier to germinate than many herbs, parsley thrives in our cool climate. The thick root of the turnip-rooted variety makes an excellent substitute for celery in soups.

When to Plant–Parsley is slow to germinate so it is wise to wait until the soil is warm. We plant around June 1.

What to Plant–We grow the single-leaf variety because we prefer the texture and taste to the more easily available double type. The turnip-rooted variety has to be ordered from a seed company.

Soil Preparation–Prepare a wide bed with one inch of manure or sludge with five pounds of wood ashes per 50 feet of bed. Fork and rake smooth until the soil is lump-free. Since parsley seed is small, the soil must be carefully prepared.

Planting–Plant parsley seed directly in the garden. It will not transplant. Make three one-quarter inch drills in the wide bed and sow the seeds evenly. Only a few feet of bed is enough for the average family's needs. Water in, and cover with a mulch and keep moist until the seed germinates. If you plant in June, the seeds will germinate in about two weeks.

Culture of Growing Plants–One inch of water a week should be enough to keep the plants supplied. Thin to three inches when they are an inch tall.

Harvest and Storage–Pick the outer leaves once the plants are growing vigorously. They will go on making new growth until fall. Parsley is a biennial so you can harvest a small crop the second year before it goes to seed. Dig the turnip-rooted kind as the need arises. If well-mulched, the roots will keep in the ground through the winter.

To have a winter's supply of leaves, hang small bunches of plants upside down from the ceiling a few inches apart. After the plants are dry, strip the leaves from the stems and store in a tightly closed glass jar.

PEAS

Introduction—Peas are worth raising because of their sweet flavor when freshly picked from the vine. Who can find such peas in the store let alone any fresh peas at all?

When to Plant—Since our summer weather is cool, peas can be planted to mature all through the growing season. The earliest planting should be about April 15 and the latest about June 15. The pea plant is hardy, but the flowers are tender to frost so the last harvest will be at the end of September.

What to Plant—Of the several varieties we have tried, Wando yields over the longest period of time. It is unaffected by the hot weather we sometimes get in June.

Soil Preparation—Peas like a cool, moist, rich soil so, if possible, add three inches of compost to the bed, if you are breaking heavy soil that has not been gardened before. If the ground is soft from previous cultivations, add one inch of sludge or manure. Be sure to include ten pounds of wood ashes per 50 feet of bed. Peas have a heavy need for the elements found in this useful material. If peas have not been grown in the bed before, the soil should be inoculated with nitrogen-fixing bacteria specific to peas. Coat peas with vegetable oil and shake them in a bag with the inoculant, which can be bought from most seed companies. Or you can substitute a small quantity of soil from ground in which peas have previously grown. Make a narrow bed for either one or two rows of peas.

Planting and Transplanting—If the ground is dry, soak it a couple of days before planting. With a hoe or wheel hoe, make a two-inch deep ditch down the middle of the bed. Drop in one seed per inch and immediately cover with moist soil. With this spacing you do not need to thin the plants. You can plant two rows of peas six inches apart and sow seeds every two inches, but the results are the same with either method; with one row, however, you avoid the extra labor of the second trench. Before covering the planting with a heavy mulch, you should provide some kind of support for the vines to grow on. Small branches or shrubs stuck in the ground are excellent, and they are free too. Put them close enough together so that they touch. The dwarf varieties need no staking, for the mulch will hold them up.

If you want to make a more permanent (and much more expensive) trellis, use three-foot chicken wire with a two-inch mesh. Push sturdy poles into the ground every six feet and staple the wire to them. Make the end posts heavier and place them two feet in the ground.

Culture of Growing Plants–When the peas come up, separate the mulch to let them through. Add mulch as the peas grow, until it is at least six inches thick. Train the peas to the supports if they fall away. Peas need a continuous supply of moisture. Give them one inch a week until the flowers open and then increase it to two. Without enough water, peas will not fill the pod.

Pests–Powdery mildew, the only disease of peas here, is worst during the rainy season. Control mildew by not picking peas or touching the plants unless they are dry. Rats and rabbits gnaw the ends of the pods and extract the peas. They can be shot, trapped, or chased out by dogs and cats.

Harvest–Pick peas as soon as the pods fill out, but before they get tough or change color. Overripe peas are not sweet, but they should be harvested anyway. This encourages the plant to continue production. To harvest, hold the vine near the pod with one hand and pick the pod with the other. The vines are delicate and tear easily if you pull the peas off with one hand.

At their peak peas should be picked every three days. Near the end of the season leave the pods on the vine to ripen. Once they are completely dry and brown, the peas can be harvested for seed the next year.

POTATOES

Introduction—Our first attempts to grow potatoes produced nothing more than marble-sized tubers in spite of a suitable climate, rich soil, and the use of certified seed potatoes. But once we began mulching heavily with pine needles, a bumper crop was the result.

When to Plant—Potato sets should be planted about May 1. Even if the shoots are damaged by a late frost, they will quickly regrow with little setback. And when frost threatens, the mulch can be pulled over the plants.

Where to Plant—Potatoes need the coolest location you can find for them. But they should be planted where no related plants (like tomatoes or peppers) have grown for several years.

What to Plant—Use certified, disease-free sets for your first attempt at growing potatoes. Ordinary store potatoes are cheaper, but they may introduce serious diseases that will be hard to eradicate. Once you have grown a crop, you can save potatoes from healthy plants for use as sets the following year. The early red variety, New Norland, has an excellent flavor and texture. It is also resistant to scab, a disease that potatoes get in neutral soils like ours. A russet type that stores well and is also scab-resistant is Norgold Russet.

Soil Preparation—Spread one inch of rotted manure or sludge on a wide bed. Fork the manure in and rake the bed smooth. Do not use wood ashes since they are alkaline. If your soil is heavy clay, add two to three inches of sand with the manure, or, better yet, use three inches of compost to replace both the sand and manure.

Planting—With a wheel or hand hoe, dig a trench four inches deep down the middle of the bed. Plant sets a foot apart and cover with soil. (If you are using your own potatoes, plant the small, one-inch potatoes whole and cut up the larger ones into one-inch chunks which contain at least one eye each. Allow the cut edges to dry for a couple of days before planting.) Cover the bed with two inches of pine needles or other mulch. In a few weeks potato shoots should appear.

We have tried laying sets on the ground and covering them with mulch. They failed to sprout, probably because of the drying winds that sweep through the garden in May. We were equally unsuccessful when the sets in the trench were covered with compost. For our climate, the conventional soil cover is best.

Culture of Growing Plants—Potatoes are shallow rooted. They need a weekly inch of water. Once the plants start to die back, they no longer need to be irrigated.

Add more mulch if the potatoes show through. It will keep the soil cooler and prevent the potatoes from turning green. (The green part must be cut out before cooking because it contains a poisonous alkaloid.)

Harvest and Storage—Potatoes can be dug when the plants flower, but for the best yield, and for storage, wait until the tops have died back. The potatoes will then be full-sized and their skins will have toughened, making long storage possible. Dig potatoes with a fork, being careful not to stab them with the teeth, and let them dry a few hours on the ground. Then store them in a cool, dark place. Potatoes too small to eat can be used for sets the following year.

PUMPKINS

Introduction–Because of our cool climate, pumpkins need every day of the growing season to reach full size and ripeness. Pumpkins are rich in vitamin A and make a good food for chickens if greens are lacking in their diet.

When to Plant–Plant as soon as the frost danger is over, about May 20 here. Do not delay; every day lost means fewer ripe pumpkins in the fall.

Where to Plant–Plant where no pumpkins or squashes have grown for three years.

What to Plant–To insure a crop of mature pumpkins, grow an early variety. We have always used Small Sugar, which often grows a lot larger than the name indicates. Because of its sweetness, it is generally considered the best pie pumpkin.

Soil Preparation–On a narrow bed spread two inches of manure or sludge with five pounds of wood ashes per 50 feet of bed. Fork the fertilizer in and rake the bed smooth. Leave one—preferably two—adjacent beds vacant for the vines to run in. Or grow tall plants like corn adjacent to pumpkins and let the vines run underneath them.

If you grow only a few pumpkins, you might want to plant them in hills. To make a hill, spread about four inches of manure or sludge and a sprinkling of wood ashes in a three-foot circle. Fork in the fertilizer and rake smooth. Pull up dirt from outside the circle to make a ridge about five inches high. Space the hills four feet apart each way.

Planting–With a stick dig an inch-deep hole every half foot and drop a seed in each hole. Cover and keep the soil from crusting with a mulch or by frequent sprinkling. If you use the hill method, plant six seeds in each hill and thin to the two best plants.

Culture of Growing Plants–Thin the seedlings to two feet. If two vigorous plants happen to grow close together, keep them, and thin the others to create an average spacing of two feet.

Train the vines to run toward the vacant beds. From the middle of August on pick flowers as they form. By then it is too late for new fruit to mature, and all the nourishment should flow into fruit already developed.

Being shallow-rooted, pumpkins should have plenty of water. Two inches a week should be sufficient. If you use hills, water about twice as much. The roots are more concentrated and use water faster.

Harvest and Storage – Pick the fruit when they are deep-yellow. Cut the stem about one inch from the fruit. As long as a heavy frost is not likely, leave the harvested pumpkins on the ground to harden off. Pull the plants and destroy them by burning.

Store fruit on a shelf where they will not touch each other. Dampness leads to rot, so the air should be cool and dry.

Pumpkins improve in flavor if kept for a month before eating.

RADISHES

Introduction – A radish, raised in rich soil with plenty of water, will be crisp and moist all the way through.

When to Plant – Though radish seed can be sown as early as the middle of April, such early plantings are often completely destroyed by the flea beetle. By the beginning of July, however, the flea beetle has passed the peak of its activity. Also the rainy season, which usually begins about the first of July, will help supply the large amounts of water radishes need to make their best growth. So instead of fighting nature with an early planting, cooperate with her by planting after July 1. For a continuous harvest, sow a few feet of seed every week until the middle of August. If a hard frost comes in the middle of September, the last planting might not succeed, but if mild weather perseveres, then the last planting will make it.

Where to Plant – Plant radishes in a cool place.

What to Plant – Though any red variety of radish will make a good crop, we prefer White Icicle. It yields a big crop of six-inch radishes which taste as good as any red variety.

Since radish seed is viable for three to five years, buy an ounce from a seed company. The cost will be much less than if you buy small packets off the supermarket seed rack.

Soil Preparation – You can grow an acceptable radish in almost any soil by simply forking in an inch of manure, but to produce the top quality, juicy, mild, and crisp kind you should incorporate a three-inch layer of compost in the top foot of soil. (Six-week's old compost is fine if it has gone through an initial heating.) Break up any clods with the back of the fork and rake smooth. But do not remove the fibrous part of the compost. It provides a spongy medium, just right for the root to swell in.

Planting – Radishes can be sown in rows or broadcast in the bed. Whichever way is used, the plants should be close enough when fully grown to form a continuous cover. Then the soil around radishes will be shaded and cool. Space rows four inches apart in a wide bed. Dig a half-inch drill and sprinkle about three or four seeds to the inch. Cover with soil and water in deeply. If you plant by broadcasting, sprinkle the seeds evenly over the whole bed and cover. Seedlings should appear in three or four days.

Culture of Growing Plants – If the weather is hot, dry, or windy, check every day to see that the soil stays moist. Once the seedlings have their true leaves, they can be thinned. First thin to half-an-inch and then wait two weeks to see how much flea beetle damage there is, and then thin to an inch.

Radishes need a thorough soaking twice a week. With average drainage it is impossible to overwater radishes. A good soaking means two inches of water spread evenly over the whole planting. It will saturate the top foot of soil where most of the roots are located. Heavy watering must be continued until all the roots are harvested.

Pests–The only serious pest is the flea beetle, and when they are numerous radishes cannot be grown in early spring by the organic method. By planting after July 1, however, you can usually escape them.

Harvest–When the radishes pop out of the ground, they are ready to pick. Harvest them promptly. Radishes left in the ground too long become dry and bitter. Feed the greens to the livestock.

RHUBARB

Introduction–Rhubarb, given care at crucial times, will yield bountifully year after year. It is delicious either frozen or canned.

When to Plant–Plant root sections in February or March when the ground is dry enough to work.

Where to Plant–Plant where the soil warms up slowly in the spring to delay the sprouting of the plant when heavy frosts are still common. A cool location will also deepen the red color of the stems. A north-facing slope is ideal.

What to Plant–Seed companies offer several new varieties for sale, all of them good.

Soil Preparation–Since rhubarb is a perennial and is grown in one place for many years, the bed should be thoroughly prepared previous to planting. If the top soil is shallow, dig down two feet and work in six inches of compost or rotted leaves.

Planting and Transplanting–Keep the roots shaded from the sun and moist up to planting time. If you can't plant the roots immediately upon receiving them, store them in a cool, damp place. Dig a wide hole one foot deep and put three inches of sludge or manure at the bottom. Cover the fertilizer with soil. Plant the root so that it will be three inches below the surface. Pack soil around the roots and water thoroughly to eliminate air pockets.

When the plants are four or five years old, they can be divided. In early spring carefully remove the dirt from around the root and slice vertically through the center of the plant with a sharp shovel. Leave one of the halves in place without disturbing its roots and divide the other into pieces that contain one or more eyes each. Replant them immediately.

Culture of Growing Plants–During a dry spring, water heavily every week. Continue watering through the summer if the rains fail. In the late fall, spread two inches of manure or sludge over the bed. Keep the fertilizer in place in the spring to retard growth. Rhubarb that comes up too early can be severely damaged by heavy frosts. Mulch the plants heavily during the growing season to preserve soil moisture and remove flower stalks as soon as they appear.

Pests–If white grubs or cutworms are present, the newly planted roots should be protected. Remove the top and bottom from a large coffee can and sink it five inches in the ground around the root. Leave it in place unless it crowds the root.

Harvest–Do not harvest any stalks for two years after planting. From the third year on, pick only those stalks which are at least an inch thick and ten inches long. The others should be left to nourish the roots. Pick by twisting off the shoots at the base of the plant. Do not eat the leaves or feed them to animals, for they contain poisonous oxalic acid in dangerous concentrations.

SHALLOTS

Introduction–Shallots should have a larger place in the home garden. They are milder and more delicately flavored than green onions, and, being well-suited to our climate, just as easy to grow. If you like French cooking, they are indispensable. Since shallots are expensive and difficult to find, they make ideal Christmas gifts.

When to Plant–Shallots are hardy, so they can be planted from the middle of April on. They take about four months to mature.

What to Plant–Shallots can be bought in gourmet food shops or ordered from Gurney's.

Soil Preparation–Shallots do best in a soil on the poor side. Work only one inch of compost or a half inch of manure into the soil with a fork and rake out the clumps. Resist the temptation to add more compost. If the soil is too rich, growth will go to the tops. Use a wide bed for a double row.

Planting–After separating the cloves from the bulb, push them into the ground until they are just covered. They should be spaced eight inches apart each way. Give them a light mulch.

Culture of Growing Plants–During dry, hot weather an inch of water a week is adequate. In the rainy season, give up watering entirely. Shallots will rot if too wet.

Harvest and Storage–When the tops have completely dried, dig the bulbs and store in a cool, dry place in an openmesh bag so that air can circulate around them.

SORREL

Introduction—Sorrel provides fresh greens with a unique flavor almost twelve months of the year. Even in the depth of winter, after a week of mild weather, it will produce a salad-sized crop of young green leaves.

When to Plant—Sorrel seeds should be sown in May when the soil has warmed up. If fortunate enough to get some root divisions from a friend, plant them in early fall or in the spring before much top growth occurs.

What to Plant—Seed is sometimes available on store seed racks. It can also be purchased from the DeGiorgi Company.

Soil Preparation—Enrich the bed with one inch of manure or sludge and a sprinkling of wood ashes. Fork in the fertilizer and rake smooth.

Planting and Transplanting—Sorrel yields heavily so ten feet of row is sufficient. Make two quarter-inch drills a foot apart and sprinkle in the seed. Cover with soil and keep moist until the seedlings appear. If germination is uneven, fill in blank spaces with extra seedlings.

To plant divisions, dig holes every six inches with a trowel, set the plants in, pack dirt around them and water in. Keep irrigating until the plants have taken hold and are growing.

Culture of Growing Plants—Sorrel needs little care. The plants will spread and form a continuous cover. Just pick the flower stalks as they form and weed conscientiously. The plants do well on a deep bi-weekly watering until the rains start. Cover the bed with an inch of manure or sludge every fall.

Pests—Grasshoppers love sorrel, but the plants grow faster than they are eaten. In fact, sorrel planted around the edge of the garden should make an excellent grasshopper trap. Insects entering from surrounding fields will feast on the border and spare the less vigorous plants inside.

Harvest—Pick leaves when they are small and tender. The larger ones can be fed to the poultry or livestock.

SPINACH

Introduction–Because of the mildness of our climate, spinach can be grown from early spring to November. Either fresh in salads or cooked, it is a tasty and nutritious vegetable.

Where to Plant–Plant in a cool location where no spinach has grown before.

What to Plant–We have always grown Bloomsdale Long Standing, which is heat-resistant and slow to go to seed.

Soil Preparation–On a wide bed, spread one inch of manure or sludge with five pounds of wood ashes per 50 feet of bed. Fork the ground and rake smooth.

Planting and Transplanting–In a flat, sow the seeds a quarter-inch deep in rows two inches apart. Water and cover until the seeds have germinated. Thin the seedlings to two inches apart when they have their true leaves. For a continuous supply, start a flat every two weeks until August 1. Two weeks before transplanting time, slice between the plants with a spatula and water well. If possible, choose a cool, cloudy day for transplanting. Set the plants about six inches apart in the bed, water well and cover any which wilt in the midday sun.

If you wish to seed spinach directly in the garden, make three one-quarter inch drills six inches apart in a wide bed. Sow the seed, cover, water, and keep moist until the seedlings emerge. Thin to six inches apart when they have their true leaves.

Culture of Growing Plants–Give the plants an inch of water a week to encourage rapid growth. Put a thick mulch around the plants to conserve moisture and keep the soil cool. Hot, dry soil will make spinach bolt early.

Pests–Fusarium wilt, which causes the leaves to turn yellow and the plant eventually to die, is a serious problem in our garden, though it does not occur in nearby plantings. Since the fungus persists in the soil once it is established there, it is best to plant spinach in another place, if your plants get this disease.

Harvest–Use the outer leaves from the plants and they will continue to produce new shoots over a long period of time. Or you can harvest the whole plant at once. When the season is over, pull the remaining plants and burn them.

SQUASH

Introduction–Summer squash is about the easiest vegetable to grow. Regardless of how small the planting, it produces more than you can use. Winter squash is rich in Vitamin A, and it stores well for later use.

When to Plant–Plant both summer and winter squash so that it will germinate after the last spring frost. Do not delay. To ripen thoroughly for good storage and full flavor, winter squash needs every day of our short growing season.

Where to Plant–Plant where no squash has grown for three years.

What to Plant–We grow zucchini, acorn, and spaghetti squash. Acorn squash sets more fruit, grows more vigorously, and ripens better than other types of winter squash. Royal Acorn is the largest of the acorn squashes. Spaghetti squash provides a nutritious substitute for the white flour pasta of the supermarket.

Soil Preparation–Prepare a narrow bed with two inches of manure or sludge and five pounds of wood ashes per 50 feet of bed. Fork the fertilizer in and rake smooth. If you prefer to grow squash in hills, prepare a three-foot circle with four inches of manure or sludge and a sprinkling of wood ashes. Fork in the fertilizer and rake smooth. Pull up dirt to make a five-inch ridge around the circle. Space the hills four feet apart in all directions. Leave an adjacent bed vacant for the vines of winter squash to run in. Zucchini is a bush type and does not require extra space.

Planting–Plant a seed one inch deep every six inches and keep the surface moist until the seedlings emerge, in seven to ten days. For hill plantings, sow six seeds and thin to the two best plants.

Culture of Growing Plants–Plants should be thinned to an average of two feet apart. For the biggest yield, water at least an inch every week. Beginning August 1, pick all the new flowers on the winter squash since not enough time remains for the plants to mature fruit from the flowers. Also all the plant's energy is channeled into the remaining fruit.

Harvest and Storage–Summer squash is best when it is small, no more than six inches long. Oversized fruit can be stuffed with meat and baked.

Acorn squash is ready to harvest when its color changes to dark green. Spaghetti squash is ripe when it turns yellow.

Pick before a heavy frost comes. Any part that freezes will quickly spoil. If acorn squash ages for a month its flavor and texture greatly improve. Store winter squash in a cool dry place. Dampness causes it to mildew and spoil.

Pests–Squash can be infected with a bluish grey root louse or aphid which can destroy whole hills of plants. As a preventative rotate squash every year to a distant part of the garden and burn plants during cleanup.

STRAWBERRIES

Introduction – Our climate makes growing strawberries a challenge. Late spring frosts and summer drought are the chief problems. Strawberries are best planted in a small area which can be given lots of attention.

What to Plant – Since strawberry blossoms are often killed by late spring frosts, grow hardy, ever-bearing varieties which will give you late summer berries when the spring crop has been lost.

If you get your plants from a friend, be sure to choose healthy, vigorous plants. Strawberries are subject to diseases which can easily destroy your planting if your transplants are not chosen carefully. You can trust plants purchased from nurseries because they are grown from virus-free stock.

Where to Plant – Choose a north-facing slope or other cool location where flowering will be delayed to miss late spring frosts. Make sure no strawberries have grown there for at least three years.

When to Plant – Strawberries are traditionally planted early in the spring while they are still dormant, but if some good plants are offered to you later in the season, do not hesitate to try them. We have successfully transplanted strawberries even in mid-summer.

Soil Preparation – Strawberries do best when grown in a rich soil full of humus. If your soil is heavy clay, fork in three inches of compost on a wide bed. Break up clumps with a hoe or rake. For soils with good texture, incorporate a one-inch layer of manure or sludge (with five pounds of wood ashes per 50 feet of bed) into the bed.

Planting – Keep each plant damp until safely in the ground. With a trowel or spade dig a hole every 18 inches down the center of the bed. Build a mound of dirt in the center of the hole and spread the roots of a plant over it. Carefully pack dirt around the roots. The crown of the plant should be level with the ground. If too high, the roots will dry out; if too low, the plant will rot. Raise a ridge of dirt around each plant and water in with about a quart of water.

Culture of Growing Plants – Young plants are easily killed by drought during the spring, so irrigate every week until the rainy season comes. Timely watering is the key to successful strawberry growing in our climate. We lost many plants until we discovered this fact.

Established berry plants also need plenty of water especially when the fruit are forming. Their roots are shallow, extending only through the top foot of soil, so keep this layer moist. Water every week.

Cultivate the bed when the weeds are small. When mature, they will be difficult to remove without uprooting the strawberries.

Some gardening books recommend complicated ways of training strawberries, but just letting them fill in the spaces in the bed produces good results with a minimum of effort. When the bed is completely full and the plants are crowding each other (this takes two or three years) the bed should be dug and the plants reestablished in a new location where strawberries have not grown for at least three years.

In the fall cover the plants with an inch of manure or sludge. This should provide sufficient cover to protect plants when the temperature does not stay below zero for protracted periods. If the winters are severe, cover the plants with an additional six inches of pine needles or straw. The mulch can be left in place the following spring, but the pine needles or straw should be pulled back.

Pests–Though the strawberry is not bothered much by insects, it is attacked by several diseases. The best control is immediately to destroy any plant that has a bad color or is not vigorously growing.

But in spite of your best efforts disease sometimes spreads through your planting. Then you should start again in another part of the garden with disease-free plants.

Harvest–Pick fruit when they are completely red but still firm and bright. Remove the deformed and overripe fruit to keep the harvest coming.

SUNFLOWERS

Introduction – Sunflowers produce a good crop in our climate. They are exceptionally high in protein and are excellent poultry (as well as human) food.

When to Plant – Because of our short growing season, sunflowers should be planted as early as possible. Every day lost reduces the harvest. Fortunately, young sunflowers have some frost resistance, so they can safely be planted here as early as May 15.

Where to Plant – Plant at the north end of the garden where the tall plants will not shade the rest of the garden.

What to Plant – The commonly available variety is Mammoth Russian, which makes a huge head with large seeds. (The top-heavy plants can topple over. If your garden is exposed to heavy winds, prop the plants with poles.)

Soil Preparation – Put down two inches of manure or sludge with five pounds of wood ashes per 50 feet of bed. Use a narrow bed for one row of plants. Fork the fertilizer in and rake smooth.

Planting – Make a one-inch hole every six inches, drop a seed in and cover. The seedlings should be up in ten days. Thin to one plant every 18 inches.

Cultivation of Growing Plants – The young plants should have one inch of water a week. Later when they have rooted deeply, they can have two inches every two weeks, part of which the normal summer rains should supply. Sunflowers, because of their large leaf surface use a lot of water, so do not neglect irrigating.

Pests – Ants occasionally eat the flowers. The best control both for the small black ant and the large, red variety is the horned toad. Whenever you find one, put it in the garden. Birds eat the ripe seeds, so harvest the heads promptly.

Harvest and Storage – When the outer seeds begin to fall out and the face of the head becomes convex, it is time to harvest. Cut off the heads with a knife and let them dry thoroughly before removing the seeds. If used for poultry food, don't bother to remove the seeds. Just give the chickens the whole head.

SWISS CHARD

Introduction–Chard is a nutritious biennial that grows vigorously even in hot weather. It is delicious sauteed in butter or steamed.

When to Plant–Chard plants should be started in the house about April 1 for transplanting out May 1. The latter is the earliest date for seeding directly in the garden.

What to Plant–Forkhook of Lucullus are the usual varieties.

Soil Preparation–See beets.

Planting and Transplanting–Sow two rows of seed one-half inch deep in a wide bed. Keep the bed moist until the seeds germinate. For extra early greens, start chard indoors about April 1. Fill small cans with potting soil, sow three or four seeds in each, and keep moist until the seedlings appear. Thin to one plant when the seedlings have their true leaves. Transplant to the garden May 1 and water daily until the plants resume growing. You should have some greens to harvest two weeks after transplanting.

Culture of Growing Plants–Thin the plants to eight inches when a few inches tall. At first, water deeply every week. Then two inches every other week should be enough.

Harvest–Pick the outer leaves as needed. You should get some early cuttings the second year before the plants go to seed.

TOMATOES

Introduction—Our first efforts to grow tomatoes in New Mexico were disappointing. From 50 plants we harvested about 50 ripe tomatoes, and they were small and tasteless. It wasn't until we found the right variety and planted it against the south side of our house that we produced a crop of large, ripe and tasty fruit. So if you live where the days are cool and the nights in the low 50's you must grow tomatoes where the sun's heat is artificially intensified by a wall or building. If no wall or building is available, you can easily make a three-sided heat trap out of boards.

When to Plant—Because of our short growing season, tomatoes should be started indoors two months before the date for transplanting. We try to set them out by May 1 with protection against the nightly frosts.

Where to Plant—Choose the hottest location available.

What to Plant—Of the many early varieties we have tried, only the Earlibell from Gurneys has produced good-sized, fully ripe fruit which mature early. Plants do not peter out but continue to form fruit all summer long.

Soil Preparation—Tomatoes have a strong, vigorous root system so they will do well even in poor, shallow soils. Incorporate one inch of manure or sludge with five pounds of wood ashes into a wide bed.

Planting and Transplanting—Large tomato sauce cans make ideal containers for starting tomatoes. Remove the top of the can and punch two holes on the sides near the bottom. Cover the bottom with small gravel for drainage. Fill to within one-half inch of the top with potting soil, and pour boiling water over the dirt to prevent damping off. Tomato seedlings are very susceptible to this fungus disease, which kills the plant by attacking the stem at ground level.

Plant seeds one-quarter inch deep, water, and cover with plastic. Place the cans in a warm place, and the seeds should germinate within ten days to two weeks. When the seedlings emerge, immediately uncover the cans, and move them to a sunny window. In a cool house like ours, the plants grow slowly for the first month, but then they really take off. When one month old, place the plants in the cold frame where they will benefit from the full sun and harden off during the cool nights. If the temperature looks as if it will go below 20 degrees, cover the cold frame with blankets or bring the tomatoes in the house. At first, one watering a day will suffice, but when the roots fill the can, they need two daily waterings, especially during hot weather.

To transplant, place the stem of the plant between two fingers and gently pull. The root ball should slide out intact. If not, turn the can upside down and rap the edge on a solid surface. In the prepared bed dig holes 18 inches apart. Make them deep enough so that the soil will come up to the first set of true leaves on the stem. Drive a five-foot stake two feet in the ground beside each plant. We use old aluminum tent poles. Water plants every day for a week. Then water every week, unless the plants wilt.

Culture of Growing Plants—Once established, tomatoes need about one inch of water a week. Underwatering will make the plants wilt and cause blossom end rot; too much causes them to grow too many leaves and not make enough fruit.

As the plants develop, tie the stems to their stakes with old pieces of rag. Held off the ground, the fruit will ripen more evenly and will not rot.

Pests—In our garden tomatoes are almost disease-free. If you find cutworms in the soil, place collars around the transplants. The collars should extend one inch in the ground and two inches above. You might have an occasional tomato horn worm, a large green larva with a big appetite for tomato leaves and fruit. Hand pick and crush.

Harvest and Storage—Observe which plants have the earliest ripe fruit and which bear the most over the longest period of time. These plants will provide seed for next year. Let a good, well-shaped fruit from each of the two or three best plants fully ripen on the vine. Pick them and scoop out the jelly and seeds, and let the gelatinous mass sit in a bowl of water for a few days until it begins to ferment. Then separate the seeds, wash them and let them dry. Store the seeds in an envelope in a cool, dry place. By this simple process you will have improved your seed for the next year's planting.

When the weather turns cold in the fall, and the plants will be damaged by the frost even when covered, pick all the fruit and keep them indoors on a sunny window sill. A few of the green ones will rot, but most will ripen and you will have fresh tomatoes until the end of November.

Pull out and burn the old plants when frost finally kills them.

TURNIPS

Introduction – If planted after the flea beetle season, turnips grow rapidly, making grapefruit-sized roots which are still solid and moist even after long storage in the ground.

When to Plant – In some years you can get away with a spring planting, but usually flea beetles will devour the whole row. So it is best to wait until July 1.

Where to Plant – Plant in a cool location.

What to Plant – The standard variety Purple-top White Globe does well here. If you only want turnip greens, plant Shogoin.

Soil Preparation – Use a wide bed for two rows of turnips. Put down one inch of manure and five pounds of wood ashes per 50 feet of bed. Fork and rake the bed smooth.

Planting – Dig two quarter-inch deep drills one foot apart. Sow about four seeds to the inch in the drills. Cover and keep moist until the seeds germinate, in about three days.

Culture of Growing Plants – Thin the seedlings in stages to a final spacing of four inches. The greens can be eaten or fed to the animals. Turnips need one inch of water a week.

Pests – Both the harlequin bug and flea beetle attack the turnip. Hand pick the former conscientiously. Flea beetles can be captured in great numbers on honey-covered pieces of cardboard.

Harvest and Storage – Start pulling every other plant when the roots are about two inches thick. Mulch the remaining plants heavily when heavy frosts come, and they will keep in the ground until the first of December. Any left then should be dug and stored in a root cellar. The intense cold of December and January will destroy the roots.

www.ingramcontent.com/pod-product-compliance
Lightning Source LLC
Chambersburg PA
CBHW051659040426
42446CB00009B/1217